Great Bike Rides,
In and Around
Winston-Salem

Great Bike Rides
In and Around
Winston–Salem

by Judi Lawson Wallace and Ken Putnam, Jr.

Photography by Christine Rucker
Cartography by Drew McCarthy

John F. Blair, Publisher
Winston-Salem, North Carolina

The paper in this book meets the
guidelines for permanence and
durability of the Committee on
Production Guidelines for
Book Longevity of the
Council on Library Resources.

DESIGN BY DEBRA LONG HAMPTON

COVER DESIGN AND TEXT COMPOSITION BY DEB BALDWIN

Library of Congress Cataloging-in-Publication Data

Wallace, Judi Lawson.

  Great bike rides in and around Winston-Salem/by Judi Lawson Wallace and
Ken Putnam ; photography by Christine Rucker ; cartography by Drew McCarthy.
      p.   cm.

  ISBN 0-89587-198-X (alk. paper)

  1. Cycling—North Carolina—Winston-Salem Area—Guidebooks. 2. Winston-Salem
Area (N.C.)—Guidebooks. I. Title: Great bike rides. II. Putnam, Ken. III. Title.

GV1045.5.N752 W569 2000
917.56'67—dc21   00-021500

Dedication

We dedicate this book to our long-time friend Gene Gillam, who has never had a bad day, or if he did you'd never know it. He is always cheerful, enjoying whatever ride he's on. And does he ever know where to ride! Gene knows all the backroads in five or six counties and introduced us to many of the rides in this book.

A modest and soft-spoken man, Gene is not one to boast about his accomplishments, so many who know him never realized he was a World War II hero. He flew more aerial combat missions during that war than any other pilot, and he lived to remember it. During his time in France, he learned to speak French and maintained a life-long interest in reading the language.

Judi recalls the time she and Gene rode to East Bend. While they were refreshing themselves in front of the old store on Main Street, they struck up a conversation with one of the older gentlemen there. The old gent was commenting on how old he was and that he didn't know how we cyclists could manage to ride those long distances. Gene turned to him and asked how old he was. The old gent replied, "I'm sixty-eight." "Well," responded Gene, "I'm seventy-two."

So, Gene, we appreciate all you've done for us over the years and all the fond memories we've accumulated together. Many of the routes in this book wouldn't be here if it hadn't been for your willingness to share the joy of cycling with others.

Table of Contents

Acknowledgments

Our greatest support for this endeavor came from Christine Rucker and Drew McCarthy. Christine gave up a great deal of time, including several Sunday mornings, to provide us with splendid professional photographs for the book. Being a cyclist herself, she has a wonderful appreciation of the vehicle and the joy it provides those who ride it. Her photographs convey this joy in a delightful fashion, and we appreciate everything she has done to make this book look great.

A wonderful carpenter by trade and an avid cyclist by avocation, Drew gave up his nights and weekends for this project, and we'll be eternally grateful to him. He purchased a new computer and software, so he could turn out wonderfully detailed and artistically attractive maps. If he ever gets tired of carpentry, he's certainly found his second calling.

In addition to thanking Drew for his cartography, Ken wants to thank him for being such a helpful and involved volunteer with both the Hearts Racing Club and Ken's Bike Shop. Drew has helped Ken organize and officiate at local bike events since the first Danbury Hill Climb in 1979. Without Drew's help, most of the local events that Ken directs would not happen.

We also appreciate the financial support of the Forsyth Tourism

Development Authority, which underwrote the research, map design, and photography for this project. We are grateful to the Winston-Salem Convention and Visitors Bureau for their assistance. We especially want to thank Stephan Dragisic, who never passed up an opportunity to plug the book.

Thanks for their help also goes to the following people and organizations:

* Bruce Heye, who looked after Judi and helped in many ways—cooking dinner, doing yard work, helping with research and offering strong arms and a warm heart for much-needed moral support.

* Our families, who showed interest and support throughout this intense project.

* Jerry Blizard and Gene Holt for their tutelage in Ken's early years in cycling.

* Lewis Newton, who asked Ken many years ago to do a different ride every Sunday. That request caused Ken to begin thinking of routes, which led to the exploration of all these different routes.

* Alan Norman, who came up with many of our rides. He and his wife Wanda have been great riding companions since the early 1980s. Alan is Mr. Smooth on a bike.

* Dennis McNeal, Randy Reavis, Brent Rocket, Wacell Waters, David Averil, Duke Weeks, Kerry Shields, Lyn Pitson, Randy Shields, Randy Adams, and all the other regular Sunday riders, whose names would fill a book. Thanks for making the Sunday rides with Ken so enjoyable.

* Greg Bean and Guy Spear, who have been Ken's early-morning riding partners—when they could get him out of bed. These guys have done their best to help Ken get his bad knees into shape each year, so he could lead the Sunday rides.

* Janet York Rolison, Penny Ender, Kathy Pounds, Roland Kreuger, and others who rode with Judi on many of these rides and offered moral support over the years.

* Mike and Linda Hastings, for providing the map and directions for

the tour around Belews Lake.

* Randy Reavis for the "Eva Cranfill Ride."

* Alan Norman for the "Lost Loop," "Farmington with Pudding Ridge Ride," and many others.

* Charlie Williams for the "Bakery Store Ride."

* Randy Shields for his training loop.

* Loretta Barren of the Winston-Salem/Forsyth County Planning Board for her thoughts about routes and for supplying information on the greenways.

* Everett Lineberry, Raymond Burcham, and Richard Horn of East Bend for graciously allowing us to photograph them on their favorite bench on Main Street in East Bend.

* Tom McGuire, Kerry Shields, Kenin Soyars, Mary Johnson, Lynn Pitson, Jim Whitler, John Anderson, Randy Reavis, Randy Adams, Pat Roberts, Kate Mewhinney, David Averill, David Todd, Alan Norman, Louis Newton, D.B. Weeks, Byron Goode, Ronnie Hudspeth, Ryke Edwards, Blair Palmer, Carolynn Berry, Aric Wilhelm, Drew McCarthy, and Kitt Goode for riding when we needed them for photographs. Some of them even rode back up a hill, so Christine could get the shots she needed.

We apologize to our friends who suggested rides that we didn't use. Traffic conditions and publication deadlines restricted the number and kinds of rides we could include.

Many other people helped behind the scenes, giving us encouragement, advice, information, and moral support. We hope we haven't forgotten anyone. If we have, please forgive us and know that your efforts were nonetheless appreciated.

Introduction

Cycling in the Piedmont

Located between the mountains and the coastal plain, the Piedmont region of North Carolina is fantastic for cycling. The terrain is varied, the scenery is beautiful, the choice of routes is extensive, and it's just plain fun. The weather is great for cycling almost year round. And, there's no better way to stay in shape that hopping on your bike for a few minutes or a few hours. The Piedmont's rolling terrain will keep you fit. We have a great time riding here and hope you'll enjoy the benefit of our many years of cycling experience.

All the routes in the book have been time-tested by many cyclists. Ken and/or Judi have ridden most of these routes many times. A few rides were recommended by cycling friends. We have tried to show you the best rides that Winston-Salem and the surrounding area have to offer. So, now it's up to you to get on your bike and ride.

The rides in the "Bike Routes" section are grouped with their starting point. Since most of them start from The Oaks Shopping Center, you will find the first rides journey in and around the East Bend community. The second grouping crosses the Yadkin River, heading toward Yadkinville. The final grouping travels around the Tanglewood Park area.

Moving from the rides that begin at The Oaks Shopping Center, the next grouping starts out of Ken's Bike Shop. The final tour travels around Belews Lake.

Under the "Family Rides" and "Mountain Bike Trails" sections, the rides follow a geographical pattern running from northwest to northeast. At the end of the book, you will find an appendix that arranges the routes from the shortest to the longest in riding distance.

About the Rides

Some of these tours are urban, but most are in rural areas. Some follow—either partially or completely—North Carolina or Forsyth County's signed bike routes. Where this happens, the signed bike-route numbers are included in the text along with the road name and state-road numbers. Although most of the rides are loops, some are out-and-back to minimize the distance where there are limited alternatives for a return route.

The rides range in length from about 2 miles for family rides to about 70 miles for more advanced cyclists. They offer something for every level from beginners to advanced veteran cyclists. All the routes listed under "Bike Routes" are on paved roads and were selected with touring bikes in mind. There are optional side trips or alternative routes you can select, depending on your level of energy and experience. The routes listed under "Mountain Bike Trails" are all in public parks.

Each ride includes a map; information on length, terrain, and where to find food; a general description of the ride; and detailed mile-by-mile directions. Since many of the rides start at the same hub, you'll find general directions to those starting points described below.

About the Starting Points

The Oaks Shopping Center in Lewisville

Most of the rides start west of Winston-Salem in the town of Lewisville, mainly because that's where local cyclists have been meeting for twenty years. As Winston-Salem grew and traffic increased, it became necessary to find a location that was away from traffic and yet close to the most popular places to ride. When an informal group started riding from Lewisville before it became a town, the local shopping center was called Sunny Acres. The starting point is now called The Oaks Shopping Center. Fortunately, the town of Lewisville is working on plans to encourage bicycling even more, so the shopping center should continue to be a good starting point for many more years.

HOW TO GET THERE

If coming from the east, take U.S. 421 west of Winston-Salem to Exit 184 at Lewisville. Turn east and The Oaks Shopping Center is less than half a mile on your left.

Coming from the west, take U.S. 421 east to Exit 184 at Lewisville. At the top of the ramp, turn left onto Williams Road and go to the stop sign at the intersection with Concord Church Road. Turn left and cross the bridge over U.S. 421. The Oaks Shopping Center is less than a half mile on your left.

An alternate route, especially if you're cycling, is to ride west straight out Country Club Road, which is off Silas Creek Parkway. When you come to a fork with Styers Ferry Road and Shallowford Road, take the right fork, which becomes Shallowford Road. Continue on Shallowford Road, straight through the heart of Lewisville. The Oaks Shopping Center will be on your right at the intersection of Williams and Shallowford Roads.

Ken's Bike Shop in Reynolda Village

Ken's Bike Shop, owned and operated by Ken Putnam, Jr., is open 10 A.M. to 5:30 P.M., Tuesday through Saturday. Ken and his staff are available to answer questions about the routes in this book, as well as other rides. Please feel free to come by for suggested rides that might match your riding skills.

HOW TO GET THERE

Ken's Bike Shop is located in Reynolda Village. The village is an upscale shopping area, housed in buildings that were originally part of the R.J. Reynolds estate. To get to Reynolda Village, drive north on Silas Creek Parkway to Wake Forest Road. Just before the entrance to Wake Forest University, make a quick right onto Reynolda Road. The village will be on the left. Go to the first traffic signal and turn left into the village. You'll make a left turn just past the median. Turn right into the parking lot beside the barn. Ken's Bike Shop is located on the lower level of the main barn.

From downtown Winston-Salem, go west on Reynolda Road. You'll pass the main entrance to Reynolda House Museum of American Art on your right. Turn right at the traffic signal into Reynolda Village. Follow the same directions as above once in the village.

Tanglewood Park

Tanglewood Park is a 1,300-acre recreation area, which was originally the estate of Will Reynolds and his wife. Will was the brother of R.J. Reynolds, founder of Reynolds Tobacco Company. Because Will and his wife had no children, they left their estate to Forsyth County at their deaths. There is an admission fee of two dollars per car or bike.

HOW TO GET THERE

Take I-40 west of Winston-Salem to Exit #182, the Tanglewood exit. At the end of the ramp, turn south onto Harper Road and go to the traffic signal at the intersection with U.S. 158. Turn right on U.S. 158. The entrance to Tanglewood Park is about 0.4 mile on your left.

Centre Stage Shopping Center in Walkertown

Walkertown is a community located in the northeast corner of Forsyth County.

HOW TO GET THERE

If coming from the west, take Business 40/U.S. 421 east to Exit 8 for U.S. 158, which heads toward Walkertown and Reidsville.

If coming from the east, take Business 40/U.S. 421 west to Exit 9 (Linville Road). At the end of the ramp, turn right on Old Greensboro Road. Travel to the intersection with U.S. 158. Turn right at the traffic signal and travel 5 miles on U.S. 158. When U.S. 158 intersects N.C. 66, turn left at the traffic signal. The Centre Stage Shopping Center will be on your left.

Starting points for "Family Rides" and "Mountain Bike Trails" will be described with each ride.

> *Neither John F. Blair, Publisher nor the authors assume any liability for accidents happening to, or injuries sustained by, readers who engage in the activities described in this book.*

Judi's Riding Tips

The Right Equipment

One of the best things about cycling is that you don't need a lot of fancy gear, but some basics will make your rides safer and more enjoyable.

•**Helmet**—A helmet is absolutely essential for your safety. Make sure you wear one that fits properly and has a secure strap. To really provide protection for your brain if you have an accident, you should wear the helmet so the front comes almost to your eyebrows.

•**A Bike That Fits**—Make sure you are riding the right size bike and that your seat is positioned properly. Here's how to tell if your bike fits right. When you're in the saddle with both feet on the pedals, place one pedal at the lowest position. The leg on that pedal should be only slightly bent. If the seat is too low, your legs will tire quickly; if it's too high, you might injure your knees. In either case, you'll have difficulty handling the bike properly.

•**Check Out Your Bike**—Check your tire pressure, brakes, handlebars, cables, and reflectors to make sure that everything works properly before you get ten miles into the country.

•**Water**—This liquid is a must any time of year, but particularly in the hot, humid summer months. Always drink before you're thirsty and consume at least a pint of water every hour. Bike shops carry water bottles and holders that can attach to your bike frame.

•**Bike Lock**—A strong lock is essential if you plan to leave your bike for sightseeing or other stops. It's important to secure both wheels and the frame to an immovable object.

•**Clothing**—You can wear just about anything to ride a bike as long as it won't get caught in the chain or other bike parts and cause you to be thrown off the bike. For longer rides, padded cycling shorts or tights prevent chafing and won't bunch up while you ride. Jerseys and jackets of lightweight materials that wick water away from your skin are especially helpful when you ride in colder weather. Padded gloves also protect your hands from numbness or from scrapes if you should fall.

•**Bike Computer**—These neat gizmos that clip to your handlebars will help you track mileage and directions. They're available in local bike shops. Although they are useful tools, they can be a distraction on group rides. When riding with a group, either turn the computer off or leave it at home.

•**Cellular Phone/Repair Kit**—If you do run into problems, a lightweight cell phone in your bike bag can be a big help. Of course, you should carry emergency numbers with you. If you don't have a cell phone, carry a small repair kit or at least a spare tube, tire irons, and a frame pump.

•**Bike Bags**—You might also want to have a small seat bag, which is ideal for carrying tools and pocket change. A handlebar bag with a clear pocket on top is handy for keeping maps and directions in front of you as you ride.

•**Glasses/Sunglasses**—Good eye protection can be important for keeping bugs and debris out of your eyes while you're riding. Preventing harm from ultraviolet rays is a consideration, too, especially if you're riding for several hours.

The Roadway

The routes in this book have been selected because they usually have minimal traffic. However, conditions change. It's up to you to be alert for potholes, debris on the road, construction projects, and other road hazards. Especially in the summer months, you might want to call ahead to find out about road construction and conditions before starting your ride.

Look Around You

Always be conscious of your surroundings, particularly if you're riding alone. Use your rearview mirror and check ahead to anticipate problem situations or conditions. Consider carrying a cell phone and/or riding with a friend or a group.

Visibility

Because of shadows and the angle of the sun, cyclists can be difficult for motorists to see in early morning and late evening. Take special care at these times. At all times, remember that drivers are looking for other vehicles, so act like one. If safety dictates it, ride farther out in the lane so you're more visible to drivers. This is especially true on the few sections of these routes where there are four lanes. Always signal your intention to turn or change lanes, so motorists can react properly.

Railroad Tracks

Always maneuver so you cross railroad tracks at a right angle. Otherwise, you risk injury if your bike slides out from under you. If one cyclist goes down, there is a risk of other cyclists crashing as well. Cyclists aren't too happy with another rider who causes a crash.

Ken's Rules of Cycling Etiquette

Introduction

When I started riding in Winston-Salem over twenty-five years ago, I was lucky to ride with friends like Gene Gillam, Mel Murray, and Jerry Blizard. They were accomplished riders and were unselfish about teaching the proper etiquette for riding in a double paceline, a single paceline, or just with a buddy.

Unfortunately, a lot of new riders don't have the same kind of instructors. I encourage those of you who are experienced riders to take an easy day and help a friend learn to ride with a group safely and harmoniously. Meanwhile, here are some hints to make shared rides more enjoyable for all. When you ride with others, you must always back off your individual riding needs for the enjoyment and responsibility of riding in a group.

Basic Common Sense Dos and Don'ts

1. Obey all traffic laws. In North Carolina, as in many other states, a bicycle is subject to the same rights and responsibilities as a motorized vehicle.

2. Use hand signals. Let other riders and motorists know your

intentions. Riding predictably is the best way to prevent crashes.

3. Stop at stoplights. Yes, those signals apply to bicyclists, because bicycles are legally classified as vehicles.

4. Don't pass cars on the right. If cars are stopped for a stop sign or signal, do not pass them on the right to get ahead. This is a major pet peeve of motorists. Instead, wait your turn like the vehicle operator you are.

5. Wear flashy clothes and visible colors for your protection. Motorists need to see you. Besides, you look much cooler. "Dress for respect."

6. Keep hand and finger gestures to yourself. You and your bike may weigh two hundred pounds, but a truck and driver weigh several tons. You won't have good odds if you take them on one-on-one. You don't need to upset anybody while you're on a bike—just give a friendly wave.

The Leader's Responsibility

1. Control the pace.

The pace at which the group is riding should be based on the muscle pressure it takes to ride. Bicycle computers should not determine the pace. The pace should slow on an uphill, increase as the hill is crested, and increase even more on the downhill.

2. Never coast on a downhill.

If the lead rider coasts on a downhill, everyone behind will have to brake the entire downhill. Because gravity causes lighter riders to go uphill more quickly and downhill more slowly than heavier riders, lighter riders should leave the front or work hard on the downhills. Conversely, larger riders should come off the front on an uphill climb, so lighter riders can control the pace at that point.

3. Point out hazards.

Front riders are responsible for pointing out road hazards, upcoming turns, approaching cars or runners, or anything that might cause a problem for anyone in the paceline behind. Here are some examples of front commands:

• Point down and yell "pothole" or "gravel" if you see such an obstacle.

• Point down and yell out "road kill" if you see dead animals in the road.

• Use an arm signal and yell "right turn" or "left turn" before the group gets to the location of the actual turn.

• Stick out your arm and hand and yell "slowing down" or "slow" when approaching a hazard or intersection.

• After looking both ways, yell "clear" or "all clear" when leading the group through intersections. If the intersection is not clear, yell "car."

4. Don't speed up.

Speeding up after making a turn or crossing an intersection is the easiest way to lose riders. Riders in the back of the paceline should yell "riders off back" or "back" if any fellow riders drop out of the paceline.

Group Riding

Riding with a group provides many social and safety benefits. When you're learning to ride, the group can teach you proper riding techniques. You'll also discover routes and sights you might otherwise never have known. When a group gets together for a ride, it is most important to have a ride leader who can listen to the other riders and figure out the pace. The leaders also need to decide if two or more groups are needed, and where the ride will go.

Unfortunately, it seems that all groups will have one or two individuals who will try to force the pace to prove they are the strongest riders. Others may try to change the route to take control of the ride. These individuals are the worst enemies of group riding. Their tactics cause the group to string out along the route or lose riders at the back.

One of the most frustrating experiences for new riders is being left to ride alone. This may cause riders to make the wrong turns, get lost, and in general, have a bad time.

We like to ride in a controlled group that keeps the riders together. For the stronger riders, we explain the route before the ride and designate a point at which they can "show their stuff" by riding in hard. The rest of the group can come in at its own pace.

You may want to leave your computer at home, so you can just enjoy the group by starting and finishing with them.

Riding in a Double Paceline

1. A double paceline is a group of riders who ride side by side in an organized manner. The pace should be comfortable for the weakest rider in the group. You should also discuss the pace before the ride. It may be better to form more than one group to compensate for different riding abilities.

2. Riding in a double paceline is a great setup for social riding. It's a good way to talk and ride. However, riders must learn to talk while looking forward. Do NOT look at the person you're talking to. Instead, watch the wheels of the riders in front of you. You can easily talk and listen while looking ahead.

3. Do NOT overlap wheels in a paceline. If you go down, so will others behind you.

4. Leave enough room between your front wheel and the rear wheel of the rider ahead of you. Change your position in the paceline if you don't trust the rider in front of you.

5. One group of riders should not hog the lead or "camp out at the front." Before the ride starts, the group should discuss how long the front rider will ride in front on a hill. This is called deciding the "length of pulls." It is recommended that the leader should not pull for more than a half-mile.

6. The pace is controlled by the outside or left front rider in the paceline. The front rider is also responsible for peeling off or dropping to the back of the paceline when the pull is through.

7. The pull should always carry a hill, which means the front rider should always stay in front until he or she has crested the hill. Front riders should never peel off before cresting a hill for two reasons. First, interrupting the pace while on a hill will create an accordion effect and may cause a crash. Secondly, visibility is poorest just before the group crests the hill.

8. The pace of the group should not accelerate to accommodate the riders coming off the front. Instead, riders coming off the front should slow down and move to the back of the paceline as soon as possible. As riders pull back, the group will be four abreast. NOTE: lead riders should pull out toward the centerline before slowing and going to the back of the paceline.

9. You should not drink, eat, spit, or blow your nose until you pull off the front and move to the back—another reason for short pulls.

10. Riders in the back of the paceline should alert others when a car is approaching or passing by yelling "car back." If a rider drops off the back, they should yell "rider off the back."

Riding in a Single Paceline

1. A single paceline is a group of riders who ride single file. In a single paceline, the lead rider pulls off to the right or left before moving to the back. No one should pull off to a different side from what is customary for the group. This point should be discussed before the ride starts. In most touring pacelines, the lead rider pulls out to the left, slows down to let the group pass on the right, and then goes to the back.

2. The length of each pull should be consistent in time, length, and pace.

3. Keeping their riding skills in consideration, riders should keep a

good gap between their front wheel and the wheel they are following. This keeps riders from colliding with the cyclists in front and causing a crash.

4. The etiquette used to point out hazards and show respect for your fellow riders is the same as for a double paceline.

Riding in Pairs

1. It is always a great idea to ride with someone. It helps to motivate both of you and is a lot safer. If you have a riding partner, you're more apt to ride regularly. You will also have someone to assist you if you run into a problem.

2. You should follow the same riding techniques as those for a single paceline. Sometimes you can ride side by side if traffic is light, but always be considerate of motorists and ride in a single file if traffic is behind you. It is legal in North Carolina to ride two abreast, but it is annoying to motorists who are following you. As cyclists, we can gain more respect if we show courtesy to our fellow highway users.

Bike Routes

East Bend—Out and Back

Starting point
The Oaks Shopping Center in Lewisville

Distance
23.4 miles

Terrain
Rolling, with a few hills

Food and drinks
The Oaks Shopping Center; East Bend

Recommendations
This is a great short ride.

Description of the route

A very popular ride in this area, this pleasant out-and-back route seems to take you back in time. Once you cross the Yadkin River and turn right on Taylor Road, you return to the rural North Carolina of times past.

Mile-by-Mile Directions	Distance to Next Turn	Total Distance
From The Oaks Shopping Center, turn LEFT on Shallowford Road (SR 1001) and ride to Conrad Road (SR 1305).	1.0	1.0
Turn RIGHT on Conrad Road and continue to Yadkinville Road (SR 1561).	2.2	3.2
Turn LEFT on Yadkinville Road, which becomes Old 421 (SR 1605) after crossing the Yadkin River. Continue on Old 421 to Taylor Road (SR 1567).	0.6	3.8
Turn RIGHT on Taylor Road and go to Flint Hill Road (SR 1549).	2.0	5.8
Go STRAIGHT on Flint Hill Road, CROSS N.C. 67, and continue to the stop sign at Main Street (SR 1545) in East Bend.	6.4	12.2
Turn LEFT on Main Street. Turn around after a rest stop. Go RIGHT on Pauline's Street, then CROSS N.C. 67 where the road name changes to Flint Hill Road. Ride to Old 421.	6.8	19.0
Turn LEFT on Old 421/Yadkinville Road and travel across the Yadkin River to Conrad Road.	1.2	20.2
Turn RIGHT on Conrad Road.	2.2	22.4
Turn LEFT on Shallowford Road and travel to The Oaks Shopping Center on the right.	1.0	23.4

Most of Forsyth County used to look this way before shopping centers and suburban developments sprang up like mushrooms.

Although you could turn right on Flint Hill Road from Old 421, you will have an easier climb if you take Taylor Road instead. After riding for 5.8 miles, you come to Flint Hill Road. From the ridge along Flint Hill,

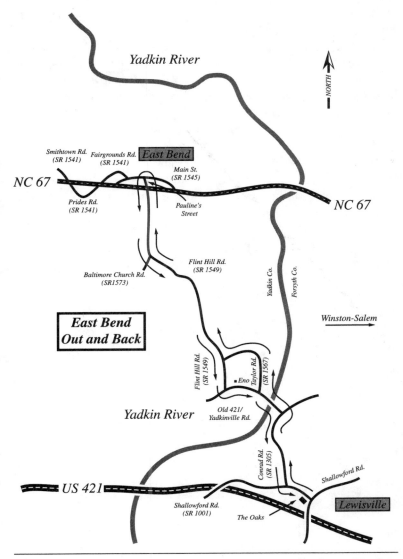

Yadkin River

Smithtown Rd.
(SR 1541)   Fairgrounds Rd.   East Bend
                (SR 1541)
NC 67   Main St.
                               (SR 1545)   NC 67
Prides Rd.   Pauline's
(SR 1541)   Street

                        Flint Hill Rd.
                        (SR 1549)
Baltimore Church Rd.
(SR1573)

East Bend
Out and Back

Yadkin Co.   Forsyh Co.

Winston-Salem

Flint Hill Rd.
(SR 1549)   Taylor Rd.
              Eno   (SR 1567)

Yadkin River   Old 421/
                Yadkinville Rd.

                        Conrad Rd.
                        (SR 1305)   Shallowford Rd.

US 421   Lewisville
            Shallowford Rd.
            (SR 1001)   The Oaks

NORTH

you have wonderful views of surrounding pastures, farmland, and even Winston-Salem on a clear day.

The turnaround point is in downtown East Bend at the old country store, which unfortunately is now closed. Local farmers and townsmen, many sporting necessary and practical overalls, usually populate the wooden benches in front of the store. Over the years, they've grown accustomed to having cyclists dressed in eccentric and colorful clothing stop for a rest break and a drink. Strike up a conversation, and you're likely to hear some of the community's history.

If you need restroom facilities, you'll want to stop at the convenience store on N.C. 67, almost directly behind the country store. It offers a wider selection of merchandise, but nowhere near the local color. Rest up a bit and enjoy the ambience before making the return trip to Lewisville.

Baltimore Road Loop

Starting point
The Oaks Shopping Center
in Lewisville
Distance
23.0 miles
Terrain
Rolling, with some good
climbs
Food and drinks
The Oaks Shopping Center
Recommendations
This is a good ride to take in
the early spring.

Description of the route

Yadkinville Road takes you
across the Yadkin River, where the
road name becomes Old 421.
Here you will enter a pastoral setting. However, new houses are
springing up in the midst of soybean and cornfields along Taylor
Road, so it's hard to say how long

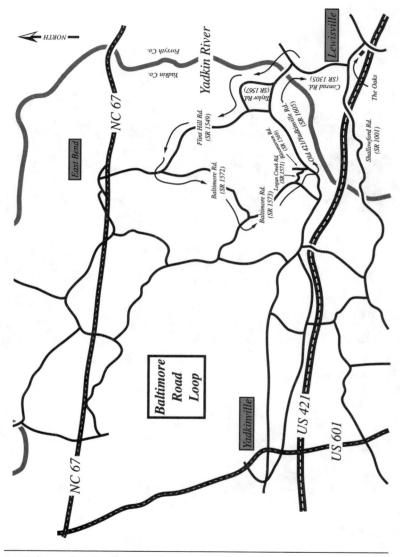

NORTH

Yadkin River

Forsyth Co.
Yadkin Co.

NC 67

East Bend

Lewisville

Conrad Rd.
(SR 1305)

Taylor Rd.
(SR 1567)

Flint Hill Rd.
(SR 1549)

Old 421/Yadkinville Rd.
(SR 1605)

The Oaks

Baltimore Rd.
(SR 1572)

Logan Creek Rd.
(SR 1571)

Binkley Rd.
(SR 1569)

Shallowford Rd.
(SR 1001)

Baltimore Rd.
(SR 1573)

Baltimore
Road
Loop

Yadkinville

US 421

US 601

NC 67

this area will remain essentially rural. Between the new houses, you'll pass barns and fields sporting farm implements as you climb higher on this winding road.

Flint Hill Road runs along the ridge, so it's mostly level as it snakes along pastures and clusters of homes. Instead of going on into the community of East Bend, this route turns onto Baltimore Road, which is also curvy and primarily level for 2.5 miles until it takes a downhill course. The view of trees and forests across the pastures is beautiful, particularly in the fall. Once past the creek, the route climbs through woods. Watch out for walnuts in the road in late summer and fall.

Immediately after the turn onto Logan Creek Road, you'll start a climb that curves through another wooded area. Forbush Elementary School is on the left at the intersection of Bloomtown Road, just before you reach Old 421 where you turn for home.

Mile-by-Mile Directions	Distance to Next Turn	Total Distance
From The Oaks Shopping Center, turn LEFT on Shallowford Road (SR 1001) and ride to Conrad Road (SR 1305).	1.0	1.0
Turn RIGHT on Conrad Road and continue to Yadkinville Road (SR 1561).	2.2	3.2
Turn LEFT on Yadkinville Road, which becomes Old 421 (SR 1605) after crossing the Yadkin River. Continue on Old 421 to Taylor Road (SR 1567).	0.6	3.8
Turn RIGHT on Taylor Road and to Flint Hill Road (SR 1549).	2.0	5.8
Turn RIGHT on Flint Hill Road and go to Baltimore Road (SR 1572).	4.1	9.9
Turn LEFT on Baltimore Road and ride to the stop sign at Cornelius Road (SR 1572).	3.8	13.7

Mile-by-Mile Directions	Distance to Next Turn	Total Distance
Turn RIGHT on Cornelius Road, which changes to Forbush Road (SR 1570). Continue on Forbush Road to Baltimore Road again.	0.2	13.9
Turn LEFT on Baltimore Road and travel to Logan Creek Road (SR 1571).	1.5	15.4
Turn LEFT on Logan Creek Road and ride to Bloomtown Road (SR 1569).	0.5	15.9
Turn RIGHT on Bloomtown Road for about 50 feet, before turning LEFT on Old 421/ Yadkinville Road. Cross the Yadkin River and travel to the stop sign at Conrad Road.	3.9	19.8
Turn RIGHT on Conrad Road and go to the stop sign at Shallowford Road.	2.2	22.0
Turn LEFT on Shallowford Road and ride to The Oaks Shopping Center, which will be on the right.	1.0	23.0

Found Loop

Description of the route

This is a popular ride with many area cyclists. It's called the Found Loop because local bikers were looking for a shorter alternative to the Lost Loop ride (covered on page 31). They'd ridden past Indian Heaps Road many times while riding the Lost Loop. One day, they decided to see where this road went. The end result was the Found Loop.

With great views and peaceful surroundings, the country roads on this route help you understand why many people choose to live in this beautiful setting. Many cyclists love this route because it allows them to leave the city and high-stress jobs and renew themselves in a peaceful setting. The route travels to East Bend, which is a familiar crossroads in many of the rides in this book. East Bend serves as a gateway to many northern and western routes. It also has friendly people who often chat with bikers while they take rest breaks.

Indian Heaps, Forbush, and Baltimore Roads offer a few ups and downs as they wander through pastures, well-tended farms, and wooded areas. With a length of a little more than 40 miles, this route offers an intermediate distance for a good training ride or leisurely tour.

Starting point
  The Oaks Shopping Center in Lewisville
Distance
  30.6 miles
Terrain
  Rolling to hilly
Food and drinks
  The Oaks Shopping Center; East Bend
Recommendations
  This is a good training ride.

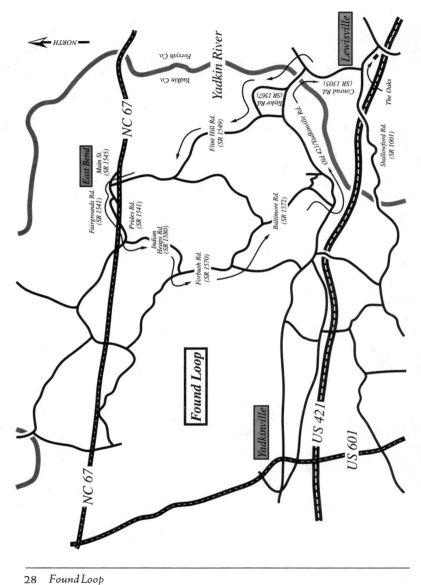

Mile-by-Mile Directions	Distance to Next Turn	Total Distance
From The Oaks Shopping Center, turn LEFT on Shallowford Road (SR 1001) and ride to Conrad Road (SR 1305).	1.0	1.0
Turn RIGHT on Conrad Road and go to Yadkinville Road (SR 1561), which becomes Old 421 (SR 1605) after crossing the river.	2.2	3.2
Turn LEFT on Old 421 and go to Taylor Road (SR 1567).	0.6	3.8
Turn RIGHT on Taylor Road and to Flint Hill Road (SR 1549).	2.0	5.8
Turn RIGHT on Flint Hill Road. CROSS N.C. 67 and continue to the stop sign at Main Street (SR 1545) in East Bend.	6.4	12.2
Turn LEFT on Main Street and go to Fairgrounds Road (SR 1541).	0.3	12.5
Turn RIGHT on Fairgrounds Road and travel to the stop sign at N.C. 67.	0.7	13.2
CROSS N.C. 67 and go onto Prides Road (SR 1541) to Indian Heaps Road (SR 1580).	0.9	14.1
Turn LEFT on Indian Heaps Road and ride to Forbush Road (SR 1570).	3.0	17.1
Turn LEFT on Forbush Road and continue to Baltimore Road (SR 1572).	3.7	20.8
Turn RIGHT on Baltimore Road and ride to the stop sign at Old 421.	2.1	22.9

Mile-by-Mile Directions	Distance to Next Turn	Total Distance
Turn LEFT on Old 421/Yadkinville Road and cross the Yadkin River to Conrad Road.	4.5	27.4
Turn RIGHT on Conrad Road and travel to Shallowford Road.	2.2	29.6
Turn LEFT on Shallowford Road and ride to The Oaks Shopping Center on the right.	1.0	30.6

Lost Loop

Starting point
The Oaks Shopping Center in Lewisville

Distance
47.1 miles

Terrain
Flat to rolling

Food and drinks
The Oaks Shopping Center; East Bend; a country store near Courtney

Recommendations
Except for moderate traffic on Conrad Road, the traffic is light. This is a beautiful ride.

Description of the route

The naming of this route has an interesting story behind it. Some local cyclists were riding in this area when they decided to take a route that bypassed downtown Yadkinville. They got lost and ended up taking this route. Thereafter, this ride was known as the Lost Loop.

This route follows one of the nicest ridge roads around. It is great for paceline riding, but riding along the ridge is nice for cyclists in any formation. The road is fairly level as you pass Fall Creek Elementary School and whiz by tobacco, soybean, and corn fields. Along Pleasant Church Road, you can see the Brushy Mountains off to the right.

East Lee Street on the outskirts of Yadkinville takes you past Willowbrook Health Care and the Unifi plant on the left. Soon thereafter, you'll see the Yadkin Correctional Center, where a mixture of satellite dishes and cows will greet you. You'll glimpse U.S. 421 through the trees on your right. Scenery consists of mown fields, littered with large round hay bales, and well-tended houses with large green lawns.

At one point, nature's own cedar farm proliferates with Christmas trees-to-be next to a dormant pasture that provides fertile ground for a variety of wildflowers and small trees. An old country store near Courtney draws locals and thirsty cyclists. Across the road, a sign with a bicycle underneath the words "Share the Road" alerts motorists to cycling activity in the area.

Take care to follow the signs for N.C. Bike Route 2 and bear left on Courtney-Huntsville Road when Farmington Road goes off to the right.

Mile-by-Mile Directions	Distance to Next Turn	Total Distance
From The Oaks Shopping Center, turn LEFT on Shallowford Road (SR 1001) and ride to Conrad Road (SR 1305).	1.0	1.0
Turn RIGHT on Conrad Road and continue to Yadkinville Road (SR 1561).	2.2	3.2
Turn LEFT on Yadkinville Road, which becomes Old 421 (SR 1605) after crossing the Yadkin River. Continue on Old 421 to Taylor Road (SR 1567).	0.6	3.8
Turn RIGHT on Taylor Road and to Flint Hill Road (SR 1549).	2.0	5.8

Mile-by-Mile Directions	Distance to Next Turn	Total Distance
Turn RIGHT on Flint Hill Road and CROSS N.C. 67. Flint Hill Road changes its name to Pauline's Street. Continue on Pauline's Street to the stop sign at Main Street (SR 1545) in East Bend.	6.4	12.2
Turn LEFT on Main Street and ride to Fair-grounds Road (SR 1541).	0.3	12.5
Turn RIGHT on Fairgrounds Road and continue to the stop sign at N.C. 67.	0.7	13.2
CROSS N.C. 67 onto Prides Road (SR 1541) and ride to the stop sign at N.C. 67. Smithtown Road will change to S.R. 1003 before reaching the stop sign.	1.3	14.5
Turn LEFT on N.C. 67 and go about 50 feet before turning RIGHT on Smithtown Road (SR 1541) to the stop sign at N.C. 67.	3.7	18.2
CROSS N.C. 67, where the road name changes to Nebo Road (SR 1570). Continue on Nebo Road to Rockford Road (SR 1510).	4.5	22.7
Turn LEFT on Rockford Road. The road number changes to 1506 at Sugartown Road. Continue on SR 1506 to the stop sign at Country Club Road (SR 1502 and 1503).	2.8	25.5
Turn LEFT on Country Club Road and ride to the traffic signal at U.S. 601 in Yadkinville.	3.1	28.6
CROSS U.S. 601 onto North Lee Avenue and go to Main Street.	0.9	29.5
CROSS Main Street on North Lee Avenue and ride to the stop sign at South State St.	1.2	30.7
STAY on South State Street, which becomes Shacktown Road (SR 1146) until you reach Old Stage Road (SR 1733).	4.2	34.9

Mile-by-Mile Directions	Distance to Next Turn	Total Distance
Turn RIGHT on Old Stage Road and pass under U.S. 421 to Watkins Road (SR 1710).	0.8	35.7
Turn LEFT on Watkins Road and ride to Courtney-Huntsville Road (SR 1001). NOTE: There is a hard left turn with a blind curve behind you!	1.7	37.4
Turn LEFT and travel on Courtney-Huntsville Road to the Yadkin River. After crossing the river, Courtney-Huntsville Road becomes Shallowford Road, but remains SR 1001. Continue on Shallowford Road to The Oaks Shopping Center on the right.	9.7	47.1

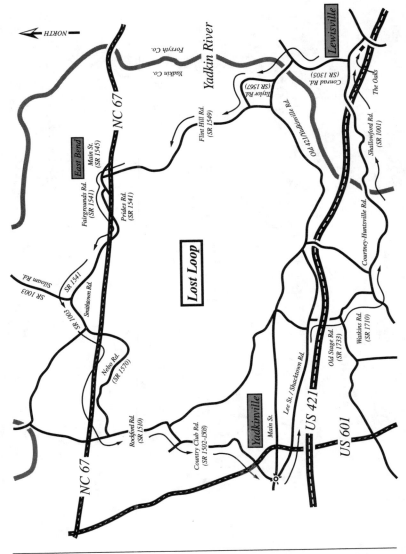

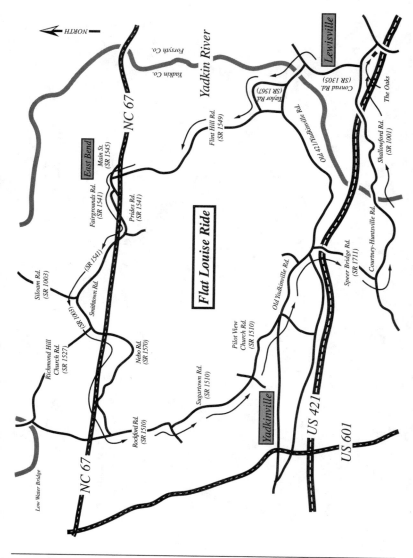

Flat Louise Ride

Description of the route

There's a story behind the name for this route. While riding along part of this route, some local cyclists were commenting about how flat it was. About that time they saw a woman sitting on her front porch. They didn't know the woman's name, but they decided they'd name the route after the next woman they met. That turned out to be a woman in the store at their rest stop. Her name was Louise.

Starting point
The Oaks Shopping Center in Lewisville

Distance
44.0 miles

Terrain
Amazingly flat in places, with some ups and downs

Food and drinks
The Oaks Shopping Center; East Bend

Recommendations
Look for Louise.

One thing you'll notice is that the road names change a lot. Every time a road crosses N.C. 67, it seems the name changes. Smithtown Road on the north side of N.C. 67 becomes Nebo Road on the other side, just after you pass Fall Creek Elementary School on the left. Nebo Road, which is pleasantly rolling with lots of pastures and fields, tends to be more open than Smithtown Road. You'll pass through the small community of Nebo before turning onto Rockford Road. Sugartown and Pilot View Church Roads eventually lead back to Courtney-Huntsville/Shallowford Road and Lewisville via Old 421 and the Speer Bridge Road connector.

Mile-by-Mile Directions	Distance to Next Turn	Total Distance
From The Oaks Shopping Center, turn LEFT on Shallowford Road (SR 1001) and go to Conrad Road (SR 1305).	1.0	1.0
Turn RIGHT on Conrad Road and ride to Yadkinville Road (SR 1561), which becomes Old 421 (SR 1605) after crossing the river.	2.2	3.2
Turn LEFT on Yadkinville Road/Old 421 and go to Flint Hill Road (SR 1549).	1.9	5.1
Turn RIGHT on Flint Hill Road, CROSS N.C. 67 and ride to the stop sign at Main Street (SR 1545) in East Bend.	6.9	12.0
Turn LEFT on Main Street and travel to Fairgrounds Road (SR 1541).	0.3	12.3
Turn RIGHT on Fairgrounds Road and ride to the stop sign at N.C. 67.	0.7	13.0
CROSS N.C. 67. The name of the road changes to Prides Road (SR 1541). Continue on Prides Road to the stop sign at N.C. 67.	1.3	14.3
Turn LEFT on N.C. 67 and travel about 50 feet before turning RIGHT on Smithtown Road (SR 1541). Continue on Smithtown Road to the stop sign at N.C. 67.	3.7	18.0
CROSS N.C. 67 onto Nebo Road (SR 1570) and ride to Rockford Road (SR 1510).	4.5	22.5
Turn LEFT on Rockford Road and go to Sugartown Road, which is still SR 1510.	2.1	24.6
Turn LEFT on Sugartown Road and ride to the stop sign at Union Grove Church Road (SR 1509).	3.2	27.8

Mile-by-Mile Directions	Distance to Next Turn	Total Distance
CROSS Union Grove Church Road and continue on Pilot View Church Road (still SR 1510) to the stop sign at Old 421.	2.3	30.1
Turn LEFT on Old 421 and go to Speer Bridge Road (SR 1711).	2.7	32.8
Turn RIGHT on Speer Bridge Road and ride to Courtney-Huntsville Road.	2.4	35.2
Turn LEFT on Courtney-Huntsville/ Shallowford Road and ride to The Oaks Shopping Center on the right.	8.8	44.0

Rockford without Rockford Ride

Description of the route

Starting point
The Oaks Shopping Center in Lewisville
Distance
34.4 miles
Terrain
Rolling to hilly
Food and drinks
The Oaks Shopping Center; East Bend
Recommendations
Enjoy the ride.

This route starts out just like the Rockford Road Loop, but it doesn't go all the way to the town of Rockford—hence the name. From the crossing at the Yadkin River, you start climbing on Taylor Road and continue to climb at the beginning of Flint Hill Road before it levels out a bit. The new houses on Taylor Road give way to open farm-land. When you reach the outskirts of East Bend the houses are closer together.

To avoid riding on N.C. 67, this route snakes across that highway several times until it reaches Nebo Road. Forbush, Baltimore, Logan Creek and Bloomtown Roads are all typical country roads with lots of curves and beautiful pastoral settings. There's little traffic on these roads, so you can enjoy the exercise and the views. Be sure to wave to farmers in their fields or people rocking on their porches.

Mile-by-Mile Directions	Distance to Next Turn	Total Distance
From The Oaks Shopping Center, turn LEFT on Shallowford Road (SR 1001) and ride to Conrad Road (SR 1305).	1.0	1.0
Turn RIGHT on Conrad Road and continue to Yadkinville Road (SR 1561).	2.2	3.2
Turn LEFT on Yadkinville Road, which becomes Old 421 (SR 1605) after crossing the Yadkin River. Continue on Old 421 to Taylor Road (SR 1567).	0.6	3.8
Turn RIGHT on Taylor Road and go to Flint Hill Road (SR 1549).	2.0	5.8
Go STRAIGHT on Flint Hill Road, CROSS N.C. 67, and continue to the stop sign at Main Street (SR 1545) in East Bend.	6.4	12.2
Turn LEFT on Main Street and ride to Fairgrounds Road (SR 1541).	0.3	12.5
Turn RIGHT on Fairgrounds Road and go to the stop sign at N.C. 67.	0.7	13.2
CROSS N.C. 67 onto Prides Road (SR 1541) and ride to the stop sign at N.C. 67.	1.3	14.5

Mile-by-Mile Directions	Distance to Next Turn	Total Distance
Turn LEFT on N.C. 67 and travel about 50 feet before turning RIGHT on Smithtown Road (SR 1541). Continue to the stop sign at N.C. 67.	3.0	17.5
CROSS N.C. 67 on Nebo Road (SR 1570) and go to Forbush Road (SR 1570).	0.9	18.4
Turn RIGHT on Forbush Road and travel to Baltimore Road (SR 1572).	6.9	25.3
Turn RIGHT on Baltimore Road and ride to Logan Creek Road (SR 1571).	1.5	26.8
Turn LEFT on Logan Creek Road and go to Bloomtown Road (SR 1569).	0.5	27.3
Turn RIGHT on Bloomtown Road and go to Old 421. Turn LEFT on Old 421/ Yadkinville Road and ride to the stop sign at Conrad Road.	3.9	31.2
Turn RIGHT on Conrad Road and continue to the stop sign at Shallowford Road.	2.2	33.4
Turn LEFT on Shallowford Road and travel to The Oaks Shopping Center on the right.	1.0	34.4

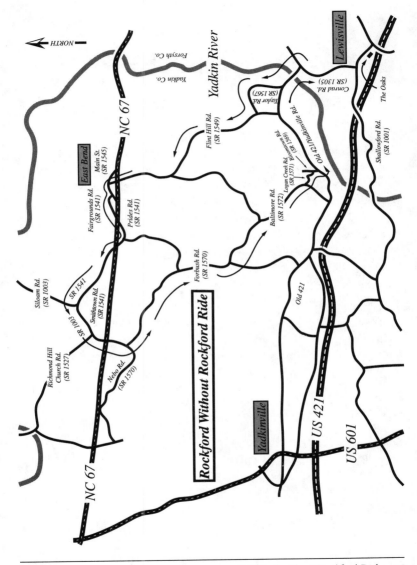

Rockford Road Loop

This route follows backroads with little traffic and great views of the mountains. Off Speer Bridge Road, you'll see signs for the large Vulcan stone quarry. You'll see that Horseshoe Road is aptly named when you pass both ends that connect to Speer Bridge Road. The moderate traffic on Old 421 is somewhat mitigated by the improved road condition. When Old 421 was resurfaced, the slightly widened roadway was a great improvement over the old concrete pavement with its regular tar ridges.

Along Pilot View Church Road, you'll confront a gradual uphill. On Sugartown Road, you will frequently see horses off to the left. In the late afternoon, the sun glows orange over the Brushy Mountains on your left.

Starting point
   The Oaks Shopping Center in Lewisville
Distance
   44.2 miles
Terrain
   Rolling to hilly
Food and drinks
   The Oaks Shopping Center; East Bend
Recommendations
   There is some traffic along Old 421.

A myriad of purple martin houses attract these helpful birds that ward off pesky insects.

The ride down to the river on Old Rockford Road is beautiful. You have wonderful views of mountains all around, with Pilot Knob off to the right. With little or no traffic, you're left to your thoughts while you pilot around the many S curves in the road. Just before the bridge, you may see longhorn cattle on your left.

After the turn, there's a hard 0.7-mile climb, but the cattle grazing nearby will offer no sympathy.

You'll make a few more climbs before you return to Lewisville and the rushed pace of suburbia.

Mile-by-Mile Directions	Distance to Next Turn	Total Distance
From The Oaks Shopping Center, turn LEFT on Shallowford Road (SR 1001) and continue to the Yadkin River. SR 1001 becomes Courtney-Huntsville Road after crossing the river. Continue on SR 1001 to Speer Bridge Road (SR 1711).	8.8	8.8
Turn RIGHT on Speer Bridge Road and ride to the stop sign at Old US 421 (SR 1605).	2.4	11.2
Turn LEFT on Old US 421 and go to Pilot View Church Road (SR 1510).	2.7	13.9
Turn RIGHT on Pilot View Church Road and travel to the stop sign at Union Grove Church Road (SR 1509).	2.3	16.2
CROSS Union Grove Church Road onto Sugartown Road (SR 1510) and continue to the stop sign at Rockford Road (SR 1510).	3.2	19.4
Turn RIGHT on Rockford Road and go to the stop sign at N.C. 67.	2.9	22.3
Go STRAIGHT on Rockford Road to the stop sign at Richmond Hill Church Road (SR 1527), just beyond the bridge. A low-water bridge is 200 yards to the left of this bridge.	2.1	24.4
Turn RIGHT on Richmond Hill Road and travel to the stop sign at Smithtown Road (SR 1003).	3.8	28.2

Mile-by-Mile Directions	Distance to Next Turn	Total Distance
Turn LEFT on Smithtown Road and go to the stop sign at N.C. 67.	2.6	30.8
Turn LEFT on N.C. 67 and travel for 50 feet before turning RIGHT on Prides Road (SR 1541). Continue on Prides Road to N.C. 67.	1.3	32.1
CROSS N.C. 67, where the road changes its name to Fairgrounds Road (SR 1541). Continue on Fairgrounds Road to the stop sign at Main Street (SR 1545).	0.7	32.8
Turn LEFT on Main Street and ride past Smitherman's Grocery to Pauline's Street.	0.2	33.0
Turn RIGHT on Pauline's Street and CROSS N.C. 67. The name of the road changes to Flint Hill Road (SR 1549). Continue on Flint Hill Road to Old 421.	6.8	39.8
Turn LEFT on Old 421 and cross the Yadkin River. Continue on Yadkinville Road to Conrad Road (SR 1305).	1.2	41.0
Turn RIGHT on Conrad Road and ride to Shallowford Road.	2.2	43.2
Turn LEFT on Shallowford Road and continue to The Oaks Shopping Center on the right.	1.0	44.2

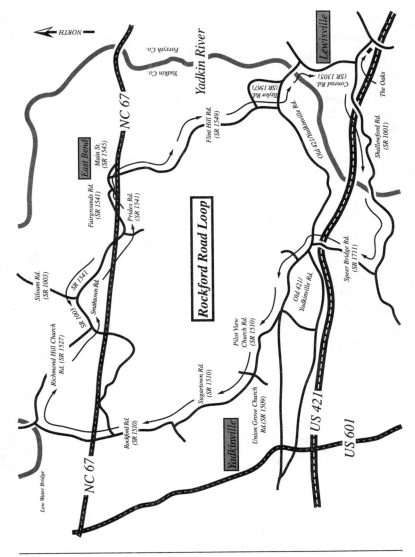

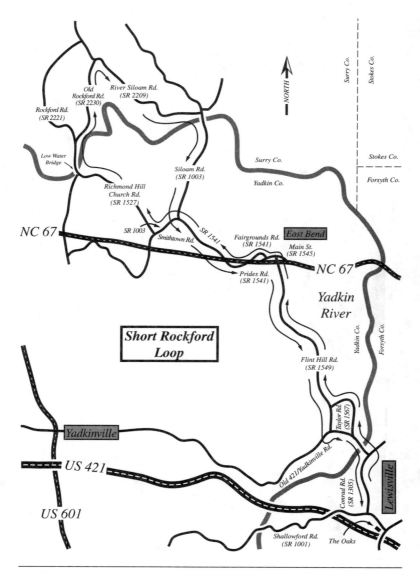

Short Rockford Loop

Description of the route

Like many of the rides in this book, this route leaves Lewisville and heads toward East Bend. The ride along Flint Hill Road offers a great view of Sauratown Mountain to the east. Locals identify this mountain by the television

Starting point
   The Oaks Shopping Center in Lewisville
Distance
   50.1 miles
Terrain
   Hilly
Food and drinks
   The Oaks Shopping Center; East Bend
Recommendations
   Get in shape before you try this one.

and radio towers atop it. Once you've passed through East Bend, take Smithtown Road. On this road, you'll have a great view of Pilot Mountain off to the right. Fall Creek Elementary School will be on your left, just before the turn on Richmond Hill Church Road.

Along Richmond Hill Church Road, you'll know you're in the foothills because you'll see mountain ranges to the north and west. Richmond Hill Park is off to the right at Limestone Road. This section of the route follows the ridge, so it's fairly level until you reach the downhill to the Yadkin River. Take care here because the low-water bridge is one-lane only and has no railings. Next, you'll enter the historic village of Rockford, where you'll take a right on Old Rockford Road. Suddenly you'll find yourself in the middle of a kudzu farm that spreads on both sides of the road. Don't stop along here or you may find yourself covered with the stuff.

River Siloam Road leads you to Siloam Road where you can cross the river. Watch out for the bad railroad tracks just after the turn onto Siloam Road. In the 1970s, a tragedy occurred here when the old Siloam bridge collapsed, killing several people who were driving across the bridge. Fortunately the new bridge is much sturdier and safer.

Mile-by-Mile Directions	Distance to Next Turn	Total Distance
From The Oaks Shopping Center, turn LEFT on Shallowford Road (SR 1001) and go to Conrad Road (SR 1305).	1.0	1.0
Turn RIGHT on Conrad Road and ride to Yadkinville Road (SR 1561).	2.2	3.2
Turn LEFT on Yadkinville Road, which becomes Old 421 (SR 1605) after crossing the river, and travel to Taylor Road (SR 1567).	0.6	3.8
Turn RIGHT on Taylor Road and go to the stop sign at Flint Hill Road (SR 1549).	2.0	5.8
Turn RIGHT on Flint Hill Road, CROSS N.C. 67 and continue to the stop sign at Main Street (SR 1545) in East Bend.	6.4	12.2

Mile-by-Mile Directions	Distance to Next Turn	Total Distance
Turn LEFT on Main Street and travel to Fairgrounds Road (SR 1541).	0.3	12.5
Turn RIGHT on Fairgrounds Road and ride to the stop sign at N.C. 67.	0.7	13.2
CROSS N.C. 67 and travel on Prides Road (still SR 1541) to another stop sign at N.C. 67.	1.3	14.5
Turn LEFT on N.C. 67 and ride about 50 feet before turning RIGHT on Smithtown Road (still SR 1541) to Richmond Hill Church Road (SR 1527).	2.6	17.1
Turn RIGHT on Richmond Hill Church Road and CROSS the river on the low-water bride and ride into the town of Rockford.	4.9	22.0
Turn RIGHT on Old Rockford Road (SR 2230) and ride to River Siloam Road (SR 2209).	3.3	25.3
Turn RIGHT on River Siloam Road, which changes back to SR 2230, and go to Siloam Road (SR 1003).	5.2	30.5
Turn RIGHT on Siloam Road and cross the Yadkin River to the stop sign at Smithtown Road (SR 1541). The road number changes when you turn onto Smithtown Road.	4.0	34.5
Turn LEFT on Smithtown Road and go to the stop sign at N.C. 67.	2.2	36.7
Turn LEFT on N.C. 67 and ride 50 feet before turning RIGHT on Prides Road. Continue on Prides Road to the stop sign at N.C. 67.	1.3	38.0

Mile-by-Mile Directions	Distance to Next Turn	Total Distance
CROSS N.C. 67, where the road name changes to Fairgrounds Road and continue to the stop sign at Main Street.	0.7	38.7
Turn LEFT on Main Street and go past Smitherman's Grocery to Pauline's Street.	0.2	38.9
Turn RIGHT on Pauline's Street and continue ACROSS N.C. 67, where the name changes to Flint Hill Road. Continue on Flint Hill Road to the stop sign at Old 421.	6.8	45.7
Turn LEFT on Old 421/Yadkinville Road and ride to the stop sign at Conrad Road.	1.2	46.9
Turn RIGHT on Conrad Road and go to the stop sign at Shallowford Road.	2.2	49.1
Turn LEFT on Shallowford Road and continue to The Oaks Shopping Center on the right.	1.0	50.1

Siloam-Rockford Loop

Description of the route

You might not realize how close Winston-Salem is to the mountains until you take this ride. As you ride along rolling Siloam Road, you'll have a great view of Pilot Mountain straight ahead. There's a nice downhill to the Yadkin River, but watch out for those bad railroad tracks. After you turn on River Siloam Road, you'll pass an imposing white house that perches on the hillside overlooking the river. As the road curves away from the river, you'll start a climb.

After you climb the hill, look for the pig statue beside the road. In fact, neighbors along this stretch of road seem to be competing for the most unusual yard art. The ups and downs on this road are rewarded by great views of the northern mountains. Although mountain vistas are off to the right, Stony Knoll Road is more rolling. This route brings you into the north end of the historic village of Rockford with a good downhill into town.

Be careful to watch the bad railroad tracks and the one-lane, low-water bridge across the

Starting point
  The Oaks Shopping Center in Lewisville
Distance
  56.6 miles
Terrain
  Rolling to quite hilly
Food and drinks
  The Oaks Shopping Center; East Bend; Rockford; a convenience store at the intersection of N.C. 67 and Siloam Road.
Recommendations
  Get yourself in shape first.

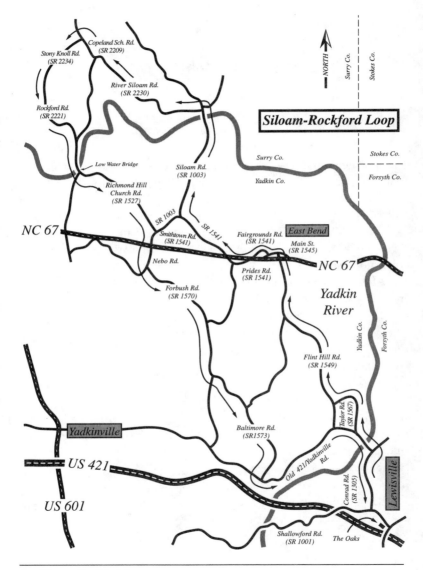

Siloam-Rockford Loop

East Bend

NC 67

NC 67

Yadkin River

Yadkinville

US 421

US 601

Lewisville

The Oaks

NORTH

Surry Co. / Stokes Co.

Surry Co. / Stokes Co.

Yadkin Co. / Forsyth Co.

Yadkin Co. / Forsyth Co.

Copeland Sch. Rd. (SR 2209)

Stony Knoll Rd. (SR 2234)

River Siloam Rd. (SR 2230)

Rockford Rd. (SR 2221)

Low Water Bridge

Richmond Hill Church Rd. (SR 1527)

Siloam Rd. (SR 1003)

SR 1003

SR 1541

Smithtown Rd. (SR 1541)

Nebo Rd.

Fairgrounds Rd. (SR 1541)

Main St. (SR 1545)

Prides Rd. (SR 1541)

Forbush Rd. (SR 1570)

Flint Hill Rd. (SR 1549)

Taylor Rd. (SR 1567)

Baltimore Rd. (SR1573)

Old 421/Yadkinville Rd.

Conrad Rd. (SR 1305)

Shallowford Rd. (SR 1001)

Yadkin River. After you cross the river, the road name changes to Richmond Hill Church Road. Forbush and Baltimore Roads are rolling roads with lots of pastureland interspersed with houses. Old 421/Yadkinville Road brings you across the Yadkin River and back to the route into Lewisville.

Mile-by-Mile Directions	Distance to Next Turn	Total Distance
From The Oaks Shopping Center, turn LEFT on Shallowford Road (SR 1001) and go to Conrad Road (SR 1305).	1.0	1.0
Turn RIGHT on Conrad Road and ride to Yadkinville Road (SR 1561).	2.2	3.2
Turn LEFT onto Yadkinville Road, which becomes Old 421 (SR 1605) when it crosses the Yadkin River. Continue on Old 421 to Taylor Road (SR 1567).	0.6	3.8
Turn RIGHT on Taylor Road and travel to Flint Hill Road (SR 1549).	2.0	5.8
Turn RIGHT on Flint Hill Road, CROSS N.C. 67, and continue to the stop sign at Main Street (SR 1545) in East Bend.	6.4	12.2
Turn LEFT on Main Street and go to Fairgrounds Road (SR 1541).	0.3	12.5
Turn RIGHT on Fairgrounds Road and continue to the stop sign at N.C. 67.	0.7	13.2
CROSS N.C. 67 onto Prides Road (still SR 1541). Travel on Prides Road to another stop sign at N.C. 67.	1.3	14.5
Turn LEFT on N.C. 67 and ride for about 50 feet before turning RIGHT on Smithtown Road (still SR 1541). Continue on Smithtown Road to Siloam Road (SR 1003).	2.2	16.7

Mile-by-Mile Directions	Distance to Next Turn	Total Distance
Turn RIGHT on Siloam Road, CROSS the Yadkin River and some difficult railroad tracks to River Siloam Road (SR 2209).	4.0	20.7
Turn LEFT on River Siloam Road, which becomes Copeland School Road (SR 2209). Continue on Copeland School Road to Stony Knoll Road (SR 2234).	6.8	27.5
Turn LEFT on Stony Knoll Road, which becomes Rockford Road (SR 2221). Continue on Rockford Road through the community of Rockford. (Watch for the railroad tracks!) Continue to the low-water bridge.	7.0	34.5
CROSS the Yadkin River on Richmond Hill Church Road (SR 1527) continue to the stop sign at Smithtown Road (SR 1003).	4.1	38.6
Turn RIGHT on SR 1003 and cross N.C. 67, where the road changes its name to Nebo Road. Continue to Forbush Road (SR 1570).	1.3	39.9
Turn LEFT on Forbush Road and ride to Baltimore Road (SR 1572).	6.9	46.8
Turn RIGHT on Baltimore Road and cross the creek to Old 421.	2.1	48.9
Turn LEFT on Old 421/Yadkinville Road and cross the Yadkin River to the stop sign at Conrad Road.	4.5	53.4
Turn RIGHT on Conrad Road and ride to the stop sign at Shallowford Road.	2.2	55.6
Turn LEFT on Shallowford Road and continue to The Oaks Shopping Center on the right.	1.0	56.6

Rockford–Siloam Reverse Loop

Description of the route

This route incorporates some of the favorite sights from several other routes. You get to ride past the old country store in East Bend and across the low-water bridge into the historic town of Rockford. You also cross over the infamous Siloam Bridge. Actually its predecessor was infamous because it collapsed in the late 1970s with several cars on it and several people lost their lives. The current stout bridge serves only as a memorial to that tragedy.

Take care as you speed down Richmond Hill Road because the road narrows to one lane just be-

Starting point
The Oaks Shopping Center in Lewisville

Distance
54.6 miles

Terrain
Rolling to quite hilly

Food and drinks
The Oaks Shopping Center; East Bend; Rockford; a convenience store at the intersection of N.C. 67 and Smithtown Road (SR 1003).

Recommendations
Get yourself in shape first.

fore you cross the narrow bridge. There are tales of cyclists approaching too fast and almost ending up in the drink. Watch the dangerous railroad tracks. It's been said that if you get to Rockford before 10 A.M. on Saturday mornings, you may be able to get a homemade fried pie at the old store/ museum.

Don't be fooled at the intersection of Rockford and Stony Knoll Roads. Rockford Road keeps straight, but the main road turns and becomes Stony Knoll Road. Stony Knoll Road is the route you want to take.

River Siloam Road parallels the river and passes in front of a majestic white house, whose hillside perch grants expansive views of the river and all who pass. Then it's back through East Bend and another possible rest stop.

Mile-by-Mile Directions	Distance to Next Turn	Total Distance
From The Oaks Shopping Center, turn LEFT on Shallowford Road (SR 1001) and go to Conrad Road (SR 1305).	1.0	1.0
Turn RIGHT on Conrad Road and ride to Yadkinville Road (SR 1561).	2.2	3.2
Turn LEFT on Yadkinville Road, which becomes Old 421 (SR 1605) when you cross the Yadkin River. Continue on Old 421 to Taylor Road (SR 1567).	0.6	3.8
Turn RIGHT on Taylor Road and travel to Flint Hill Road (SR 1549).	2.0	5.8
Turn RIGHT on Flint Hill Road. CROSS N.C. 67 and continue to the stop sign at Main Street (SR 1545) in East Bend.	6.4	12.2
Turn LEFT on Main Street and ride to Fairgrounds Road (still SR 1541).	0.3	12.5
Turn RIGHT on Fairgrounds Road and go to the stop sign at N.C. 67.	0.7	13.2

Mile-by-Mile Directions	Distance to Next Turn	Total Distance
CROSS N.C. 67 onto Prides Road (still SR 1541) and continue to another stop sign at N.C. 67.	1.3	14.5
Turn LEFT on N.C. 67 and travel about 50 feet before turning RIGHT on Smithtown Road (SR 1541). Continue on Smithtown Road to Richmond Hill Church Road (SR 1527).	2.6	17.1
Turn RIGHT on Richmond Hill Church Road and travel to the low-water bridge across the Yadkin River. CROSS the bridge on Rockford Road (SR 2221). At the 80-degree turn, Rockford Road goes straight but the main road turns and becomes Stony Knoll Road (SR 2234). Continue on Stony Knoll Road to Copeland School Road (SR 2209).	11.1	28.2
Turn RIGHT on Copeland School Road. The name of the road changes to River Siloam Road (SR 2230). Continue on River Siloam Road to the stop sign at Siloam Road (SR 1003).	6.8	35.0
Turn RIGHT on Siloam Road and go to the stop sign at Smithtown Road.	4.0	39.0
Turn LEFT on Smithtown Road and ride to the stop sign at N.C. 67.	2.2	41.2
Turn LEFT on N.C. 67 and travel 50 feet before turning RIGHT on Prides Road.	1.3	42.5
CROSS N.C. 67. The name of the road changes to Fairgrounds Road. Continue on Fairgrounds Road to the stop sign at Main Street.	0.7	43.2
Turn LEFT on Main Street and go past Smitherman's Grocery to Pauline's Street.	0.2	43.4

Mile-by-Mile Directions	Distance to Next Turn	Total Distance
Turn RIGHT on Pauline's Street and CROSS N.C. 67. The name of the road changes to Flint Hill Road (SR 1549). Continue on Flint Hill Road to Old 421.	6.8	50.2
Turn LEFT on Old 421/Yadkinville Road and cross the Yadkin River to Conrad Road.	1.2	51.4
Turn RIGHT on Conrad Road and go to the stop sign at Shallowford Road.	2.2	53.6
Turn LEFT on Shallowford Road and turn RIGHT into The Oaks Shopping Center.	1.0	54.6

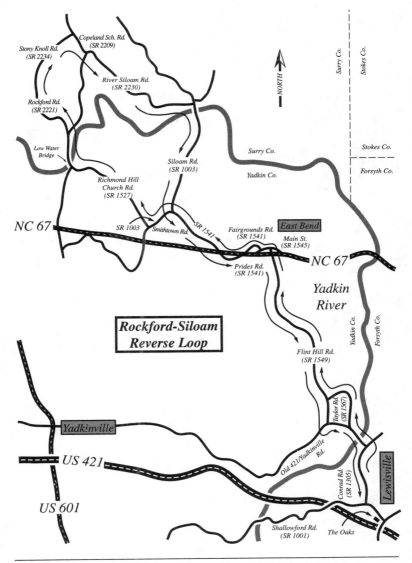

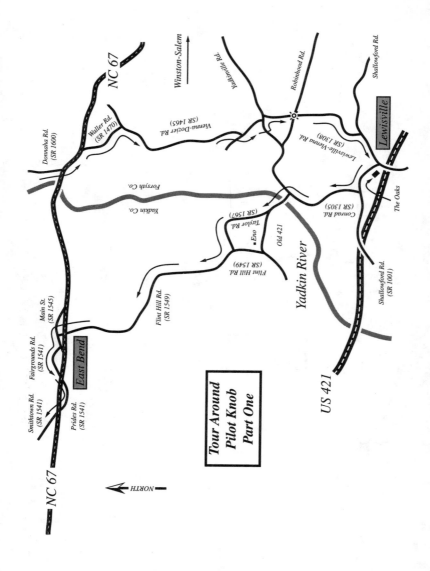

Tour Around Pilot Knob Part One

NC 67

Winston-Salem

Donnaha Rd. (SR 1600)

Waller Rd. (SR 1470)

Vienna-Dozier Rd. (SR 1465)

Yadkinville Rd.

Robinhood Rd.

Shallowford Rd.

Lewisville

Lewisville-Vienna Rd. (SR 1308)

Forsyth Co.

Yadkin Co.

Conrad Rd. (SR 1305)

The Oaks

Taylor Rd. (SR 1567)

• Eno

Old 421

Yadkin River

Flint Hill Rd. (SR 1549)

Shallowford Rd. (SR 1001)

Main St. (SR 1545)

Flint Hill Rd. (SR 1549)

Fairgrounds Rd. (SR 1541)

East Bend

Smithtown Rd. (SR 1541)

Prides Rd. (SR 1541)

US 421

NC 67

← NORTH

Tour Around Pilot Knob

Description of the route

Over the course of this ride, the wonderful 360-degree views of Pilot Knob more than compensate for distance and climbs. The first view of Pilot Knob comes on Siloam Road; it is off to your right in the distance. The terrain on Siloam

Starting point
The Oaks Shopping Center in Lewisville

Distance
56.8 miles

Terrain
Rolling, with some challenging climbs

Food and drinks
The Oaks Shopping Center; East Bend; an occasional country store

Recommendations
This tough ride circles Pilot Mountain. It is best to do it later in the season.

Road is rolling as you approach the Yadkin River. Just past the river, Hardy Road presents a significant hill with major curves— visibility is about 100 yards in front, so ride cautiously.

A big hill awaits you after a left turn by the substation on Pilot

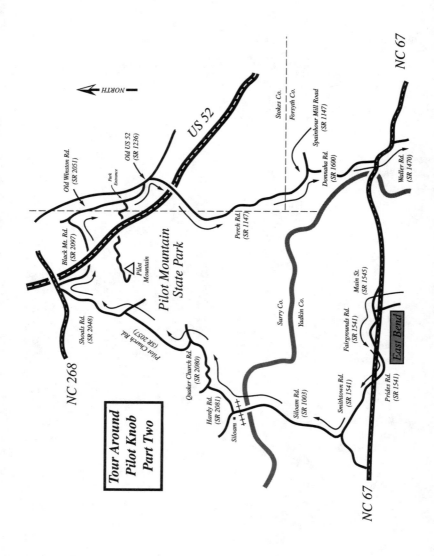

Tour Around
Pilot Knob
Part Two

NORTH

Old Winston Rd.
(SR 2051)

Old US 52
(SR 1236)

US 52

Park
Entrance

Black Mt. Rd.
(SR 2097)

Pilot
Mountain

Pilot Mountain
State Park

Shoals Rd.
(SR 2048)

NC 268

Pilot Church Rd.
(SR 2057)

Quaker Church Rd.
(SR 2080)

Hardy Rd.
(SR 2081)

Siloam

Siloam Rd.
(SR 1003)

Smithtown Rd.
(SR 1541)

Surry Co.

Yadkin Co.

Perch Rd.
(SR 1147)

Stokes Co.

Forsyth Co.

Spainhour Mill Road
(SR 1147)

Donnaha Rd.
(SR 1600)

Waller Rd.
(SR 1470)

Main St.
(SR 1545)

Fairgrounds Rd.
(SR 1541)

East Bend

Prides Rd.
(SR 1541)

NC 67

NC 67

Church Road, but you've got a great view of Pilot Mountain at the top. At this point, it looks as though the road runs right into the mountain. Thank goodness there are usually very few cars so you can enjoy the views of tobacco fields with the knob as a backdrop. The tar-and-gravel Pilot Church Road leads to Shoals Road and a view of the knob from the northwest. The route is planned so you're on N.C. 268 for a very short distance. However, you can follow N.C. 268 into Pilot Mountain proper on Main Street for an optional side trip. The town is familiar to fans of *The Andy Griffith Show* as Mount Pilot, a neighboring town to Mayberry. Pilot Knob lies straight in front of you on Old Winston Road, but keep your attention focused because some dogs live along this route. Pilot Knob Park Road (SR 1151) goes to the right, if you want to climb the 3 miles to the knob. About 4.2 miles along Perch Road, the historic Horne Creek Farm is off to the right on Hauser Road. If you're inclined to cool off in the river, you'll also see the signs for Yadkin Islands Park.

As you cross back into Forsyth County, Perch Road becomes Spainhour Mill Road. Take care as you cross the bad railroad tracks at the King water plant. Part of this route follows Forsyth County Bike Route 21 along N.C. 67. This road has high traffic, but it also has a narrow shoulder. After winding through some of the backroads of Lewisville, you'll return to The Oaks Shopping Center.

Mile-by-Mile Directions	Distance to Next Turn	Total Distance
From The Oaks Shopping Center, turn LEFT on Shallowford Road (SR 1001) and go to Conrad Road (SR 1305).	1.0	1.0
Turn RIGHT on Conrad Road and ride to Yadkinville Road (SR 1561).	2.2	3.2
Turn LEFT on Yadkinville Road, which turns into Old 421 (SR 1605) after crossing the Yadkin River, and go to Taylor Road (SR 1567).	0.6	3.8

Mile-by-Mile Directions	Distance to Next Turn	Total Distance
Turn RIGHT on Taylor Road and go to the stop sign at Flint Hill Road (SR 1549).	2.0	5.8
Turn RIGHT on Flint Hill Road, CROSS N.C. 67 and continue to the stop sign at Main Street (SR 1545) in East Bend.	6.5	12.3
Turn LEFT on Main Street and go to Fairgrounds Road (SR 1541).	0.3	12.6
Turn RIGHT on Fairgrounds Road and travel to another stop sign at N.C. 67.	0.7	13.3
CROSS N.C. 67 onto Prides Road (still SR 1541) to another stop sign at N.C. 67.	1.3	14.6
Turn LEFT on N.C. 67 and travel about 50 feet to Smithtown Road (still SR 1541). Turn RIGHT onto Smithtown Road and travel to Siloam Road (SR 1003).	2.1	16.7
Turn RIGHT on Siloam Road. Cross the Yadkin River and dangerous railroad tracks to Hardy Road (SR 2081).	3.8	20.5
Turn RIGHT on Hardy Road and ride to Quaker Church Road (SR 2080).	1.6	22.1
Turn RIGHT on Quaker Church Road and go to Pilot Church Road (SR 2057).	1.8	23.9
Turn LEFT on Pilot Church Road and ride to Shoals Road (SR 2048).	2.9	26.8
Turn LEFT on Shoals Road and travel to the stop sign at N.C. 268.	2.6	29.4
Turn RIGHT on N.C. 268 (which is also N.C. Bike Route 4) and ride to the southbound ramp for U.S. 52. The ramp is just past the Texaco station.	0.2	29.6

Mile-by-Mile Directions	Distance to Next Turn	Total Distance
Turn RIGHT on the southbound ramp for U.S. 52 and then immediately RIGHT on Black Mountain Road (SR 2097) and go to the stop sign at Old Winston Road (SR 2051).	3.4	33.0
Turn RIGHT on Old Winston Road and go to Old U.S. 52 (SR 1236).	2.5	35.5
Turn RIGHT on Old U.S. 52 and ride to Perch Road (SR 1147).	0.5	36.0
Turn RIGHT on Perch Road and travel to U.S. 52.	0.9	36.9
CROSS the bridge over U.S. 52. The name of the road changes to Spainhour Mill Road when you enter Forsyth County. Continue on Spainhour Mill Road to Donnaha Road (SR 1600).	6.9	43.8
Turn RIGHT on Donnaha Road and go to N.C. 67.	2.5	46.3
Turn LEFT on N.C. 67 and ride to Waller Road (SR 1470). NOTE: Forsyth County Bike Route 21 starts at the intersection of Waller Road and N.C. 67. Waller Road has a high volume of traffic, but there is a narrow shoulder.	0.9	47.2
Turn RIGHT on Waller Road and travel to Vienna-Dozier Road (SR 1465).	1.4	48.6
Turn RIGHT on Vienna-Dozier Road. NOTE: You are still on Forsyth County Bike Route 21. Continue on Vienna-Dozier Road to River Ridge Road (SR 1446).	3.8	52.4
Turn RIGHT on River Ridge Road and travel to the stop sign at Yadkinville Road.	0.6	53.0

Mile-by-Mile Directions	Distance to Next Turn	Total Distance
Turn LEFT on Yadkinville Road and go to Lewisville-Vienna Road (SR 1308).	0.1	53.1
Turn RIGHT on Lewisville-Vienna Road and ride to the signal at Robinhood Road.	0.9	54.0
CROSS Robinhood Road at the stoplight and CONTINUE on Lewisville-Vienna Road to the stop sign at Shallowford Road.	2.0	56.0
Turn RIGHT on Shallowford Road, which is the main street through the town of Lewisville. Continue on Shallowford Road to The Oaks Shopping Center.	0.8	56.8

Dobson Loop

You won't be on this route for long before you'll realize what foothills are. Heading toward Dobson, you're also heading toward the Brushy Mountains, and you'll have great views of these mountains as well as other local peaks. On Flint Hill Road just past Baltimore Road, you have a great view of Sauratown Mountain off to the right. On Smithtown Road, you'll see Pilot Knob on the right. Fall Creek Elementary School is on your left, just before the turn onto Richmond Hill Church Road.

Richmond Hill Church Road gives a view of mountains to the north and west, which are particularly spectacular in the fall when the sky is a clear, deep blue and visibility is good. This section of the route is mainly level because it follows the ridge. There's a nice downhill to the Yadkin River on Richmond Hill Church Road, but take care because it narrows to one lane to cross the low-water bridge.

As you enter the town of Dobson, the county seat for Surry County, you'll pass Surry Central High School and Surry Community College on your left. Service stations and convenience stores on Main Street offer

Starting point
  The Oaks Shopping Center in Lewisville
Distance
  68.0 miles
Terrain
  Rolling to hilly
Food and drinks
  The Oaks Shopping Center; East Bend; Rockford; Dobson
Recommendations
  Get in shape first!

a nice place for a rest break. At Atkins Street, the route follows N.C. Bike Route 4. This part of the ride has a fantastic view of Pilot Mountain straight ahead. As you head toward Siloam Road, watch for the llama on Turkey Ford Road. The return trip takes you back through East Bend and across the Yadkin to Lewisville.

Mile-by-Mile Directions	Distance to Next Turn	Total Distance
From The Oaks Shopping Center, turn LEFT on Shallowford Road (SR 1001) and ride to Conrad Road (SR 1305).	1.0	1.0
Turn RIGHT on Conrad Road and go to Yadkinville Road (SR 1561).	2.2	3.2
Turn LEFT on Yadkinville Road, which becomes Old 421 (SR 1605) when it crosses the Yadkin River. Continue on Old 421 to Taylor Road (SR 1567).	0.6	3.8
Turn RIGHT on Taylor Road and travel to the stop sign at Flint Hill Road (SR 1549).	2.0	5.8
Turn RIGHT on Flint Hill Road, CROSS N.C. 67 and continue to the stop sign at Main Street (SR 1545) in East Bend.	6.4	12.2
Turn LEFT on Main Street and ride to Fairgrounds Road (SR 1541).	0.3	12.5
Turn RIGHT on Fairgrounds Road and ride to the stop sign at N.C. 67.	0.7	13.2
CROSS N.C. 67 onto Prides Road (still on SR 1541) and go to the stop sign at N.C. 67.	1.3	14.5
Turn LEFT on N.C. 67 and go for about 50 feet before turning RIGHT on Smithtown Road (still SR 1541). Continue on Smithtown Road to Richmond Hill Church Road (SR 1527).	2.6	17.1

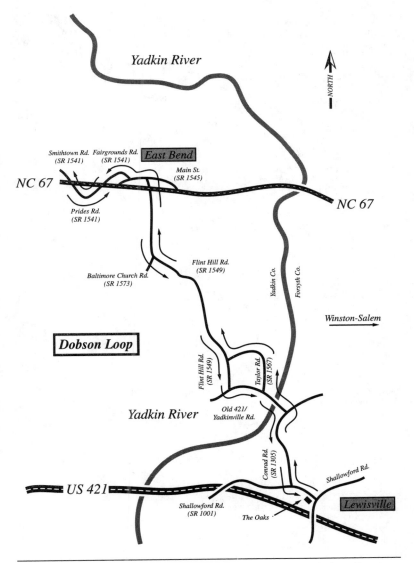

Mile-by-Mile Directions	Distance to Next Turn	Total Distance
Turn RIGHT on Richmond Hill Church Road and cross the low-water bridge and the dangerous railroad tracks and ride into town of Rockford.	4.9	22.0
Continue on Rockford Road (SR 2221) to the community of Stony Knoll and past South Surry Rescue Squad to the place where Rockford Road turns left.	4.2	26.2
Turn LEFT on Rockford Road and continue to the stop sign at the intersection with Bray Ford Road (SR 2227).	1.6	27.8
Turn LEFT on Rockford Road (SR 2221) and cross Fisher River to the stop sign at N.C. 268.	0.7	28.5
At the stop sign at N.C. 268, go STRAIGHT on Rockford Road.	3.5	32.0
At the intersection with U.S. 601, go STRAIGHT and continue into the town of Dobson to the stop at Main Street.	0.2	32.2
Turn RIGHT on South Main Street, which can be a rest stop, and ride to Atkins Street.	1.3	33.5
Turn RIGHT on Atkins Street. When you cross U.S. 601 again, the road name changes to Turkey Ford Road (SR 1100).	1.0	34.5
Go STRAIGHT on Turkey Ford Road, where you will travel up and down three hills. Continue on Turkey Ford Road to Siloam Road (SR 1003).	5.0	39.5
Turn RIGHT on Siloam Road and cross N.C. 268 to the town of Siloam. You will then travel across the railroad tracks to Smithtown Road.	12.8	52.3

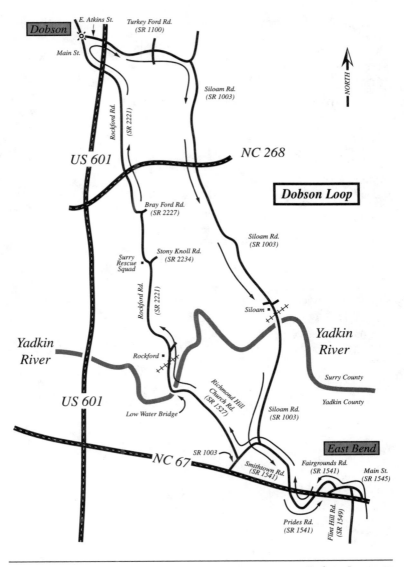

Mile-by-Mile Directions	Distance to Next Turn	Total Distance
Go STRAIGHT on Smithtown Road to the stop sign at N.C. 67.	2.2	54.5
Turn LEFT on N.C. 67 and travel 50 feet before turning RIGHT on Prides Road.	1.3	55.8
CROSS N.C. 67. The road changes its name to Fairgrounds Road. Continue on Fairgrounds Road to the stop sign at Main Street in East Bend.	0.7	56.5
Turn LEFT on Main Street and go past Smitherman's Grocery to Pauline's Street.	0.3	56.8
Turn RIGHT on Pauline's Street. CROSS N.C. 67, where the name changes to Flint Hill Road. Continue on Flint Hill Road to the stop sign at Old 421.	6.8	63.6
Turn LEFT on Old 421/Yadkinville Road and cross the Yadkin River to the stop sign at Conrad Road.	1.2	64.8
Turn RIGHT on Conrad Road and travel to the stop sign at Shallowford Road.	2.2	67.0
Turn LEFT on Shallowford Road and ride to The Oaks Shopping Center on the right.	1.0	68.0

Chicken Coop Ride

Description of the route

You can ride this route by itself or as an extension of several other rides that link to Old 421. Most cyclists prefer this route as a return for the Found Loop, Lost Loop, Rockford without Rockford, and Siloam Rockford routes. Using this return route will keep you from riding all the way back on Old 421, which has more traffic.

This route gets its name from the chicken houses you will see on the right side of Speer Bridge Road. Shallowford Road meanders through the western part of Forsyth County, which is called West Bend because the Yadkin River makes a westward turn here that is almost ninety degrees. After you cross U.S. 421, the traffic diminishes, and the setting becomes more rural. At Scott Road, you'll pass an old country store on your left, which unfortunately is now closed. Farther along the route, there's a well-maintained, very old brick house on the right. It looks like it has an underground house behind it.

The road bends toward the river for a pleasant downhill before turning uphill as it winds its

Starting point
The Oaks Shopping Center in Lewisville

Distance
21.7 miles

Terrain
Rolling to hilly in places

Food and drinks
The Oaks; a restaurant on Courtney-Huntsville Road at the intersection with Farmington Road

Recommendations
Good training ride for early in the season

...rough a nicely shaded portion of road. This section, which is in ...dkin County, is called Courtney-Huntsville Road. The next segment of the ride is on Speer Bridge Road, which is a pleasant country road that links back to Old 421 and the return route to Lewisville.

Mile-by-Mile Directions	Distance to Next Turn	Total Distance
From The Oaks Shopping Center, go LEFT on Shallowford Road (SR 1001). CROSS the Yadkin River. The name of the road changes to Courtney-Huntsville Road but remains SR 1001. Continue on SR 1001 to Speer Bridge Road (SR 1711).	8.8	8.8
Turn RIGHT on Speer Bridge Road and cross U.S. 421. Continue on Speer Bridge Road to a stop sign at Old 421 (SR 1605).	2.4	11.2
Turn RIGHT on Old 421, which becomes Yadkinville Road (SR 1561) at the river. Continue on Yadkinville Road to the stop sign at Conrad Road (SR 1305).	7.3	18.5
Turn RIGHT on Conrad Road and ride to the stop sign at Shallowford Road.	2.2	20.7
Turn LEFT on Shallowford Road and travel to The Oaks Shopping Center, which will be on your right.	1.0	21.7

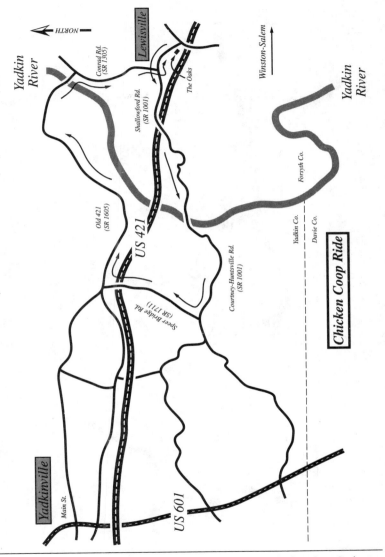

Chicken Coop Ride

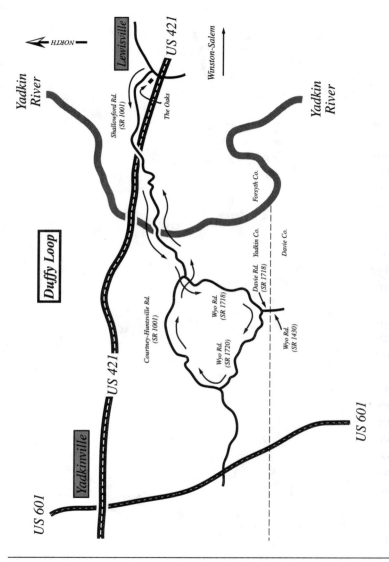

Duffy Loop

This ride is named after Mike and Patti Duffy, who live along this route. This ride is a training loop that local riders have used for twenty years. Once you get past U.S. 421, there's very little traffic, and the motorists you do meet have seen a lot of cyclists. Some good hills and fast-rolling sections will challenge you on this course.

This section of Forsyth County in the west bend of the Yadkin River offers a pleasant rolling ride. Westbend Vineyards, which takes its name from the area, is located just south of Shallowford Road on Williams Road. As you near the river, you'll see a prime real-estate section with large, elegant houses on spacious acreage.

On Wyo Road, which travels up and down with quite a few curves thrown in for good measure, you'll see very few cars and trucks. Instead, you'll see lots of woods and only scattered houses.

Starting point
The Oaks Shopping Center in Lewisville
Distance
24.8 miles
Terrain
Rolling, with good hills at the river
Food and drinks
The Oaks Shopping Center
Recommendations
Say thanks to Mike and Patti for suggesting this ride.

It's not unusual to see deer along the roadside. Toward dusk be careful that you don't collide with one that's on the way to dinner across the road.

There's also a Moonshine Road in this area. Hmmm—wonder how that road got its name? Don't be too tempted to explore. Remember you have to ride back on two wheels.

Mile-by-Mile Directions	Distance to Next Turn	Total Distance
From The Oaks Shopping Center, turn LEFT on Shallowford Road (SR 1001). CROSS the Yadkin River. The name of the road changes to Courtney-Huntsville Road but remains SR 1001. Continue on SR 1001 to Wyo Road (SR 1718).	7.3	7.3
Turn LEFT on Wyo Road and go to the stop sign at another section of Courtney-Huntsville Road.	5.8	13.1
Turn RIGHT on Courtney-Huntsville/ Shallowford Road and travel across the Yadkin River to The Oaks Shopping Center on the left.	11.7	24.8

Eva Cranfill Ride

You might think this road is named after the road that turns off Courtney-Huntsville Road. It was actually named for a schoolteacher who taught Randy Reavis, one of the local riders who found this route. It is coincidental that the ride passes by Eva Cranfill Road. You may see that road close to the first turn on this ride.

After a straight shot out Shallowford/Courtney-Huntsville Road, Ray T. Moore Road takes you past a restaurant surprise—the German Family Restaurant. As the name implies, this is indeed a restaurant owned by a German family. You will see the restaurant and a tar-and-gravel road on the left before you hit the S-curve and the downhill. Before you pass through a residential area on Old Stage Road, there's another twisting downhill.

Just before you connect a second time with Courtney-Huntsville/Shallowford Road for the return trip to Lewisville, watch for the old log house on Brawley Road.

Starting point
   The Oaks Shopping Center in Lewisville
Distance
   31.5 miles
Terrain
   Rolling, with a few hills
Food and drinks
   The Oaks Shopping Center; Courtney Grocery; Dennis Popcorn Store
Recommendations
   This is a good ride if you don't want many turns.

Mile-by-Mile Directions	Distance to Next Turn	Total Distance
From The Oaks Shopping Center, turn LEFT on Shallowford Road (SR 1001). SR 1001 becomes Courtney-Huntsville Road after it crosses the river. Continue on that road to Ray T. Moore Road (SR 1725).	13.1	13.1
Turn RIGHT on Ray T. Moore Road and ride to the stop sign at Old Stage Road (SR 1733).	2.7	15.8
Turn RIGHT on Old Stage Road and travel to Brawley Road (SR 1735).	1.5	17.3
Turn RIGHT on Brawley Road and continue to the stop sign at Courtney-Huntsville Road.	2.1	19.4
Turn LEFT on Courtney-Huntsville Road/ Shallowford Road to The Oaks Shopping Center on the right.	12.1	31.5

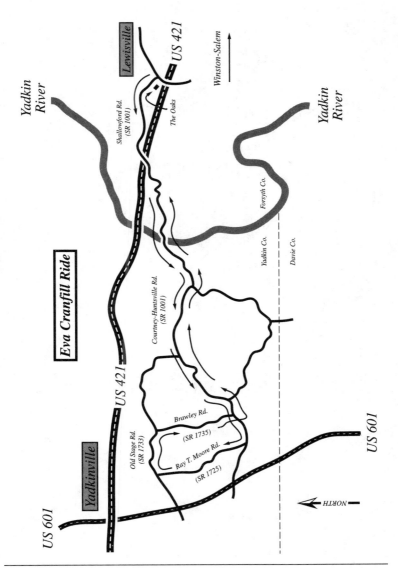

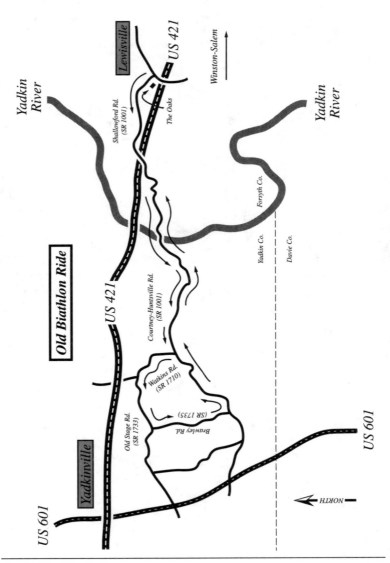

Old Biathlon Ride

Description of the route

This ride was part of the Pizza Hut Biathlon that began in 1983. The event continues today at Tanglewood Park as the YMCA Biathlon. Slightly more than a twenty-five-mile ride, it makes a good training ride. The route is rolling on either side of the river,

Starting point
   The Oaks Shopping Center in Lewisville
Distance
   26.7 miles
Terrain
   Rolling, with climbs around the river
Food and drinks
   The Oaks Shopping Center, Hollar's Grocery
Recommendations
   This is a good training ride.

but both sides also have a good descent and climb.

You'll follow Courtney-Huntsville Road almost to the community of Courtney. Hollar's Grocery is on the right, just before you reach Watkins Road. Watkins Road takes you past old tobacco barns and over Harmon Creek to Old Stage Road. Brawley Road crosses Spiker and Harmon Creeks before leading you back to Courtney-Huntsville Road. At this location, you are closer to Courtney. You'll return by the same route on which you came out. This route also happens to be N.C. Bike Route 2.

Mile-by-Mile Directions	Distance to Next Turn	Total Distance
From The Oaks Shopping Center, turn LEFT on Shallowford Road (SR 1001). CROSS the Yadkin River, where the road name changes to Courtney-Huntsville Road but remains SR 1001. Continue to Watkins Road (SR 1710), which appears just after Hollar's Grocery.	9.4	9.4
Turn RIGHT on Watkins Road and ride to the stop sign at Old Stage Road (SR 1733).	1.6	11.0
Turn LEFT on Old Stage Road and go to Brawley Road (SR 1735).	1.5	12.5
Turn LEFT on Brawley Road and go to the stop sign at Courtney-Huntsville Road.	2.1	14.6
Turn LEFT on Courtney-Huntsville/ Shallowford Road and travel to The Oaks Shopping Center on the right.	12.1	26.7

Shacktown Falls Tour

Shallowford/Courtney-Huntsville Road is a popular component of many rides in this book because it offers one of the few bridges over the Yadkin River, the western boundary of Forsyth County. Although the routes across the river are limited, there are many different roads on both sides of the river that allow you to vary your routes. This ride travels out Courtney-Huntsville to Watkins Road, just past Hollar's Grocery. A good climb on Watkins Road takes you past large chicken houses on the right.

There's another good climb on Old Stage Road, after you pass under U.S. 421. Shacktown Road also offers a good climb. You finally get a good downhill on Styers Mill Road, which has a sharp curve that sways left and then right as it parallels the creek. This fast downhill leads to a one-lane bridge over the creek. You can see Shacktown Falls to the left, just before you start a steep uphill.

When you get to Old 421, the traffic is busy, but you're going

Starting point
  The Oaks Shopping Center in Lewisville
Distance
  27.8 miles
Terrain
  Rolling to hilly, with some steep climbs
Food and drinks
  The Oaks Shopping Center; Hollar's Grocery
Recommendations
  This is not a long ride, but it has many climbs.

downhill for the most part, so you can maintain your speed. Speer Bridge Road, which crosses U.S. 421, is fairly wide and smooth. On this road, you gradually climb back to Courtney-Huntsville Road and the road to Lewisville.

Mile-by-Mile Directions	Distance to Next Turn	Total Distance
From The Oaks Shopping Center, turn LEFT on Shallowford Road (SR 1001). CROSS the Yadkin River, where the road name changes to Courtney-Huntsville Road but remains SR 1001. Continue on SR 1001 to Watkins Road (SR 1710).	9.4	9.4
Turn RIGHT on Watkins Road and travel to the stop sign at Old Stage Road (SR 1733).	1.7	11.1
Turn RIGHT on Old Stage Road and go to Shacktown Road (SR 1146).	1.2	12.3
Turn LEFT on Shacktown Road and ride to Styers Mill Road (SR 1605). Note: Styers Mill Road is S.R. 1605 until it crosses Shacktown Creek, where it becomes S.R. 1510.	0.3	12.6
Turn RIGHT on Styers Mill Road and continue to the stop sign at Old 421 (SR 1605).	1.5	14.1
Turn RIGHT on Old 421 and go to Speer Bridge Road (SR 1711).	2.5	16.6
Turn RIGHT on Speer Bridge Road and travel to the stop sign at Courtney-Huntsville Road.	2.4	19.0
Turn LEFT on Courtney-Huntsville/ Shallowford Road and go to The Oaks Shopping Center on the right.	8.8	27.8

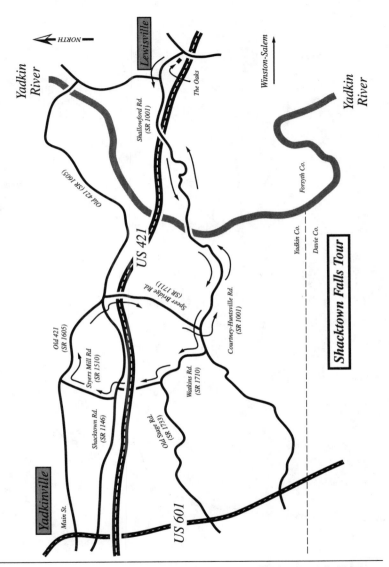

NORTH

Yadkin River

Lewisville

Winston-Salem

The Oaks

Shallowford Rd. (SR 1001)

Old 421 (SR 1605)

Yadkin River

Forsyth Co.

US 421

Yadkin Co.

Davie Co.

Speer Bridge Rd. (SR 1711)

Courtney-Huntsville Rd. (SR 1001)

Old 421 (SR 1605)

Styers Mill Rd. (SR 1510)

Watkins Rd. (SR 1710)

Shacktown Rd. (SR 1146)

Old Stage Rd. (SR 1733)

Shacktown Falls Tour

Yadkinville

Main St.

US 601

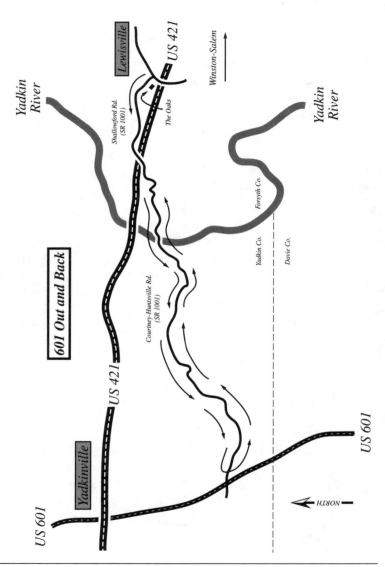

601 Out and Back

US 421

Lewisville

US 421

Shallowford Rd.
(SR 1001)

The Oaks

Winston-Salem

Yadkin
River

Yadkin
River

Courtney-Huntsville Rd.
(SR 1001)

Forsyth Co.

Yadkin Co.

Davie Co.

Yadkinville

US 421

US 601

US 601

NORTH

601 Out & Back

Starting point

The Oaks Shopping Center in Lewisville

Distance

28.8 miles

Terrain

Rolling, with a few good hills

Food and drinks

The Oaks Shopping Center; the convenience store at intersection of Courtney-Huntsville Road

Recommendations

This is a good, simple training ride.

Description of the route

This route is known as a no-brainer ride in local circles. You can't get lost on this one. It starts at The Oaks Shopping Center and follows North Carolina Bike Route 2 to the intersection with U.S. 601 in Yadkin County.

The easternmost stretch of this route travels to the river where it takes you past scattered developments, an old country store (which is now closed), Westbend Vineyards and lovely large estates. Sometimes in summer, there are signs at one of these estates advertising that you can pick your own blueberries and raspberries. Past these estates, there's a good downhill to the river, followed by a challenging climb before the road levels out. Fortunately, this climb meanders a bit and passes through a cool shady section near the crest of the hill.

The road continues to wend past pastures and planted fields. You'll pass through the small community of Courtney, where you will see the school on the right as you leave town. On the route back, watch for things you might have missed when coming from the other direction.

Mile-by-Mile Directions	Distance to Next Turn	Total Distance
From The Oaks Shopping Center, turn LEFT on Shallowford Road (SR 1001). CROSS the Yadkin River, where SR 1001 changes its name to Courtney-Huntsville Road. Continue on SR 1001 to the stop sign at U.S. 601. You should TURN AROUND at the stop sign.	14.4	14.4
CONTINUE on Courtney-Huntsville Road across the Yadkin River. Keep on Shallowford Road to The Oaks Shopping Center on the right.	14.4	28.8

Lone Hickory Ride

If you ride during the week, the Courtney-Huntsville Road offers a good source of food—the Dennis Popcorn Store is on the right after you ride 7.8 miles. The store is open Monday through Friday from 9 A.M. to 5 P.M. Otherwise, the other places listed below can provide beverages and restroom facilities. This route is popular because once you've climbed up the hill from the river, Courtney-Huntsville Road levels out nicely.

This level trend continues as you cross U.S. 601. When you cross U.S. 601, the name of the road changes to Fish Brandon Road. Renegar's Store is located where Fish Brandon ends at Lone Hickory Road. The distance calculated for this tour is based on the assumption that you will turn around when you get to the community of Lone Hickory. If you go as far as the fire station, you'll have to add several tenths of a mile to the total. Renegar's Store makes a nice spot for a break.

Starting point
The Oaks Shopping Center in Lewisville

Distance
39.8 miles

Terrain
Rolling, with a few good hills

Food and drinks
The Oaks Shopping Center; the convenience store at the intersection of Courtney-Huntsville Road and U.S. 601; Renegar's Store; Dennis Popcorn Store on weekdays

Recommendations
Ride during the week if you want popcorn.

Returning by way of Old Stage Road gives you a change of scenery. Watkins Road rolls past long, low chicken houses and fields of burley tobacco. You'll also see horses and cattle along this stretch. Be sure to wave if you see folks outside.

Mile-by-Mile Directions	Distance to Next Turn	Total Distance
From The Oaks Shopping Center, turn LEFT on Shallowford Road (SR 1001). After you cross the Yadkin River, SR 1001 changes its name to Courtney-Huntsville Road. Continue on SR 1001 to the stop sign at U.S. 601.	14.4	14.4
CROSS U.S. 601 and continue on Fish Brandon Road (SR 1165) to the stop sign at Lone Hickory Road (SR 1002) and Renegar's Store.	1.8	16.2
Turn LEFT on Lone Hickory Road and travel to the Lone Hickory community, where you turn around.	4.1	20.3
CONTINUE on Lone Hickory Road to the stop sign at U.S. 601.	4.3	24.6
CROSS U.S. 601 onto Old Stage Road (SR 1733) and go to Watkins Road (SR 1710).	4.1	28.7
Turn RIGHT on Watkins Road and travel to the stop sign at Courtney-Huntsville Road.	1.7	30.4
Turn LEFT on Courtney-Huntsville/ Shallowford Road and go to The Oaks Shopping Center on the right.	9.4	39.8

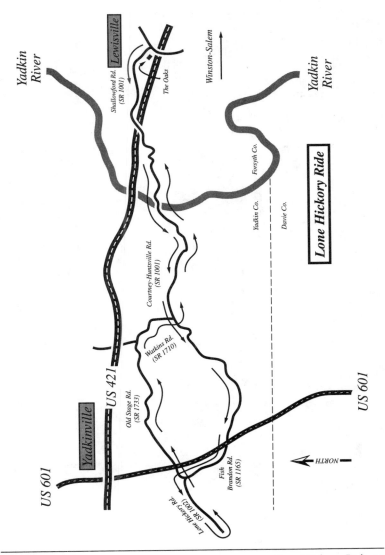

Yadkin River

Lewisville

Shallowford Rd. (SR 1001)

The Oaks

Winston-Salem

Forsyth Co.

Yadkin River

Courtney-Huntsville Rd. (SR 1001)

Yadkin Co.

Davie Co.

Lone Hickory Ride

Watkins Rd. (SR 1710)

US 421

US 601

Yadkinville

Old Stage Rd. (SR 1733)

Fish Brandon Rd. (SR 1165)

Lone Hickory Rd. (SR 1002)

US 601

NORTH

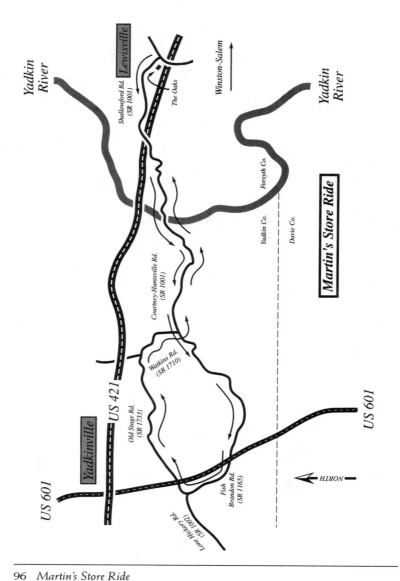

Yadkin River

Lewisville

Shallowford Rd. (SR 1001)

The Oaks

Winston-Salem

Yadkin River

Forsyth Co.

Martin's Store Ride

Yadkin Co.

Davie Co.

Courtney-Huntsville Rd. (SR 1001)

US 421

Watkins Rd. (SR 1710)

Old Stage Rd. (SR 1733)

US 601

Yadkinville

US 601

Fish Brandon Rd. (SR 1165)

Lone Hickory Rd. (SR 1002)

NORTH

Martin's Store Ride

Description of the route

There actually was a Martin's Store on the corner of Fish Brandon and Lone Hickory Roads; hence the ride's name. The store that stands there now is called Renegar's Store. It is a nice halfway point for a rest break. If you check Yadkin County on an atlas, you'll find that Martin's Store is also the name of the community around this intersection.

Lone Hickory Road takes its name from a community to the west of the intersection. We speculate that Old Stage Road was the route traveled by stagecoaches in the old days. Perhaps one of the old-timers on the route can tell you the true story behind the name.

Watkins Road's rolling surface takes you past the long, low houses of a chicken farm. Horses and cattle graze in nearby pastures. Burley tobacco, recognizable by its small leaf, is abundant here. Burley is also harvested later, so you'll still see leaves on the stalks into the fall.

A number of ranches in the area are home to Black Angus cattle, which are famous for their delicious meat. Yadkin Valley Nursery Company provides a variety of plants and shrubs for area residents.

Starting point
The Oaks Shopping Center in Lewisville

Distance
31.8 miles

Terrain
Rolling, with some hills

Food and drinks
The Oaks Shopping Center

Recommendations
This is a good medium-distance ride

Mile-by-Mile Directions	Distance to Next Turn	Total Distance
From The Oaks Shopping Center, turn LEFT on Shallowford Road (SR 1001). SR 1001 becomes Courtney-Huntsville Road after crossing the river. Continue on SR 1001 to the stop sign at U.S. 601.	14.4	14.4
CROSS U.S. 601 on Fish Brandon Road (SR 1165) and go to the stop sign at Lone Hickory Road (SR 1002).	1.8	16.2
Turn RIGHT on Lone Hickory Road and ride to U.S. 601.	0.4	16.6
CROSS U.S. 601 onto Old Stage Road (SR 1733) and travel to Watkins Road (SR 1710).	4.1	20.7
Turn RIGHT on Watkins Road and go to the stop sign at Courtney-Huntsville Road.	1.7	22.4
Turn LEFT on Courtney-Huntsville/ Shallowford Road and ride to The Oaks Shopping Center on the right.	9.4	31.8

Bunny Rabbit Loop

Description of the route

This route loops through the Farmington community to bring you back to Courtney-Huntsville/ Shallowford Road. This pleasant route got its name because it has become a tradition to ride it on Easter Sunday morning. On one of the Easter rides, some local riders saw a dead

Starting point
   The Oaks Shopping Center in Lewisville
Distance
   29.8 miles
Terrain
   Rolling, with some good climbs
Food and drinks
   The Oaks Shopping Center; the convenience store at the intersection of Farmington Road and N.C. 801
Recommendations
   This is a pleasant ride.

rabbit on Cedar Creek Road. The name evolved from that experience.

When you come to the stop sign at the intersection of Cedar Creek and Pudding Ridge Roads, the Pudding Ridge Golf Club is diagonally across the road. With sweeping vistas of pastureland complete with horses, Pudding Ridge Road is particularly pretty.

Farmington Road traverses a farming community. The principal part of this settlement clusters around the intersection of Farmington Road and N.C. 801. The convenience store here offers a good place to get a drink and rest your legs before you cross the Yadkin and climb the hills back to The Oaks Shopping Center.

Mile-by-Mile Directions	Distance to Next Turn	Total Distance
From The Oaks Shopping Center, turn LEFT on Shallowford Road (SR 1001). CROSS the Yadkin River, where SR 1001 becomes Courtney-Huntsville Road but remains SR 1001. Continue on SR 1001 to Wyo Road (SR 1718 and later SR 1430).	7.3	7.3
Turn LEFT on Wyo Road and ride to Davie Road (SR 1720).	2.9	10.2
Turn LEFT on Davie Road, which becomes Wyo Road (SR 1430), and go to the stop sign at N.C. 801.	2.6	12.8
Turn RIGHT on N.C. 801 and travel to Cedar Creek Road (SR 1434).	0.2	13.0
Turn LEFT on Cedar Creek Road and ride to Pudding Ridge Road (SR 1435).	2.5	15.5
Turn LEFT on Pudding Ridge Road and continue to Farmington Road (SR 1410).	1.2	16.7
Turn LEFT on Farmington Road and go to the stop sign at N.C. 801.	1.9	18.6
CROSS N.C. 801 and ride on Farmington Road to the stop sign at Courtney-Huntsville Road.	4.6	23.2
Turn RIGHT on Courtney-Huntsville/ Shallowford Road and go to The Oaks Shopping Center on the right.	6.6	29.8

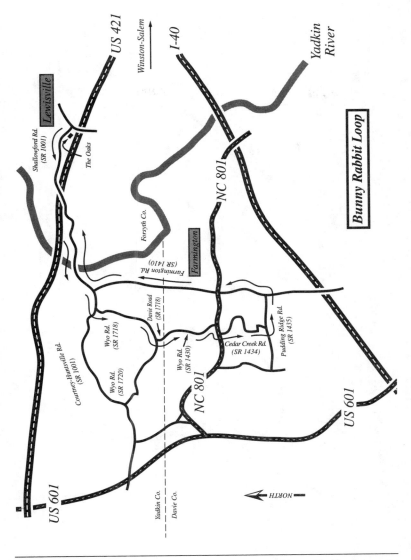

US 421

Winston-Salem

I-40

Yadkin River

Lewisville

Shallowford Rd. (SR 1001)

The Oaks

NC 801

Forsyth Co.

Farmington

Farmington Rd. (SR 1410)

Courtney-Huntsville Rd. (SR 1001)

Davie Road (SR 1718)

Wyo Rd. (SR 1718)

Wyo Rd. (SR 1430)

Cedar Creek Rd. (SR 1434)

Pudding Ridge Rd. (SR 1435)

Wyo Rd. (SR 1720)

NC 801

US 601

US 601

Yadkin Co.

Davie Co.

NORTH

Bunny Rabbit Loop

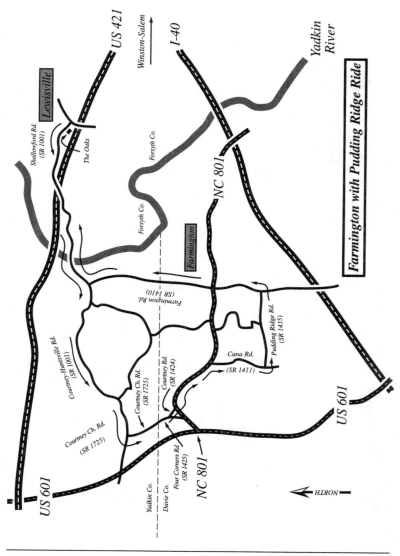

Farmington with Pudding Ridge Ride

The western section of Forsyth County along Shallowford Road is beautiful. Once you pass over U.S. 421, the scenery and sounds become much more rural. The modern bridge over the Yadkin River replaces the old steel truss bridge that stood in this spot for many years. Although many requested that the old bridge be left to one side for fishermen and cyclists, the state insisted on removing the old relic, even though the new bridge and the road leading to it were placed farther north.

The climb up the western side of the river may be long, but the many trees that shade the road make the uphill much more pleasant. After you pass Hollar's Grocery on the right, look for the large rose garden on the left that belongs to the cousin of Mr. Hollar's wife. You'll frequently see her tending the garden when the weather is conducive.

Shortly after Courtney Church Road enters Davie County, the name changes to Four Corners Road (SR 1425). The country lane provides a curvy downhill to the creek before ascending on the other side. The lands along N.C. 801 look like Christmas tree farms because there are so many cedar trees. There's also a nice climb. Cana Road leads to Pudding Ridge

Starting point
The Oaks Shopping Center in Lewisville

Distance
40.7 miles

Terrain
Up and down

Food and drinks
The Oaks Shopping Center; Dennis Popcorn Store on weekdays; Hollar's Grocery

Recommendations
This ride offers good riding conditions most of the time.

Road. On Pudding Ridge Road, you will see the Pudding Ridge Golf Course on the right. This road is also home to rolling farmland and lots of horses. Farmington Road leads you through the lovely little community of Farmington and back to Courtney-Huntsville Road.

Mile-by-Mile Directions	Distance to Next Turn	Total Distance
From The Oaks Shopping Center, turn LEFT on Shallowford Road (SR 1001). CROSS the Yadkin River, where SR 1001 changes its name to Courtney-Huntsville Road. Continue on SR 1001 to Courtney Church Road (SR 1725).	18.6	18.6
Turn LEFT on Courtney Church Road. Courtney Church Road changes its name to Four Corners Road and becomes SR 1425 when it reaches Davie County. Continue on SR 1425 to Courtney Road (SR 1424).	1.9	20.5
Turn LEFT on Courtney Road and go to N.C. 801.	0.1	20.6
Turn LEFT on N.C. 801 and ride to Cana Road (SR 1411).	2.2	22.8
Turn RIGHT on Cana Road and travel to Pudding Ridge Road (SR 1435).	2.2	25.0
Turn LEFT on Pudding Ridge Road and continue to Farmington Road (SR 1410).	2.6	27.6
Turn LEFT on Farmington Road and go to N.C. 801.	1.9	29.5
CROSS N.C. 801 and ride to the stop sign at Courtney-Huntsville Road.	4.6	34.1
Turn RIGHT on Courtney-Huntsville/ Shallowford Road and continue to The Oaks Shopping Center on the right.	6.6	40.7

Liberty Church Ride

This ride is a shorter version of the White Rabbit Ride. Instead of turning left on Joyner Road, you stay on Lone Hickory Road until you reach Liberty Church Road. The terrain on this route is level to rolling, except for the hills on the immediate sides of the river crossing.

Fish Brandon Road is narrow but fairly level as it nips alongside cornfields. You'll see an interesting mixture of old and new houses here. Large, stately oak trees greet you along Liberty Church Road. After riding about 1.4 miles on Liberty Church Road, you enter Davie County and the road number changes to SR 1002. The road gets its name from Liberty Baptist Church.

When you continue straight on Chinquapin Road, Bell Branch Road goes off to the right. Continue on Chinquapin Road until you reach the stop sign at Fish Brandon Road. This is a short distance from the intersection of Fish Brandon Road and U.S. 601. From U.S. 601, it's a fairly straight shot back to Lewisville.

Starting point
The Oaks Shopping Center in Lewisville

Distance
39.8 miles

Terrain
Rolling to hilly

Food and drinks
The Oaks Shopping Center; the convenience store at the intersection of Courtney-Huntsville Road and U.S. 601

Recommendations
Considering the distance, this is an amazingly level ride for the most part.

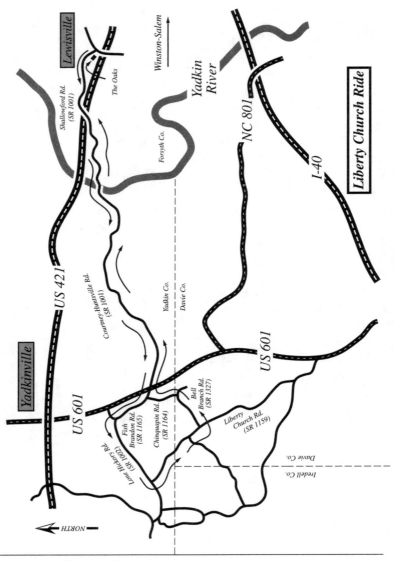

Liberty Church Ride

Mile-by-Mile Directions	Distance to Next Turn	Total Distance
From The Oaks Shopping Center, turn LEFT on Shallowford Road (SR 1001). Continue on SR 1001 to the stop sign at U.S. 601. SR 1001 changes its name to Courtney-Huntsville Road once you cross the Yadkin River.	14.4	14.4
CROSS U.S. 601. After crossing U.S. 601, the road name changes to Fish Brandon Road (SR 1165). Continue on Fish Brandon Road to the stop sign at Lone Hickory Road (SR 1002).	1.8	16.2
Turn LEFT on Lone Hickory Road and ride to Liberty Church Road (SR 1159).	3.1	19.3
Turn LEFT on Liberty Church Road and go to Bell Branch Road (SR 1327).	2.8	22.1
Turn LEFT on Bell Branch Road and travel to Chinquapin Road (SR 1164).	1.5	23.6
Go STRAIGHT on Chinquapin Road to the stop sign at Fish Brandon Road.	1.2	24.8
Turn RIGHT on Fish Brandon Road and go to the stop sign at U.S. 601.	0.2	25.0
CROSS U.S. 601 onto Courtney-Huntsville/Shallowford Road. Continue to The Oaks Shopping Center on the right.	14.8	39.8

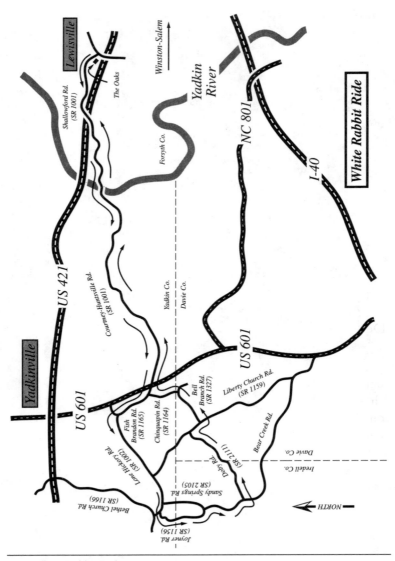

White Rabbit Ride

Description of the route

The route's name derives from a watering hole called The White Rabbit. On this route, Lone Hickory Road leads to Joyner Road, which is mostly level. When you cross into Davie County, Joyner Road's road number changes from SR 1156 to SR 2106.

When Liberty Church Road crosses from Yadkin into Davie County, the name of the road

Starting point
The Oaks Shopping Center in Lewisville

Distance
45.6 miles

Terrain
Rolling to hilly

Food and drinks
The Oaks Shopping Center; a convenience store at the intersection of Fish Brandon Road and U.S. 601.

Recommendations
You can ride this route at any time, but traffic is busy around The Oaks Shopping Center.

changes to Ollie Harkey Road (SR 1324). On this road, there's an interesting old graveyard with neat white markers, surrounded by a stone wall. This section of the ride offers rolling hills that pass through woods and beautiful green pastures.

Chinquapin Road—no doubt named for the variety of tree—leads back into Yadkin County and to Fish Brandon Road. As you approach U.S. 601, look for the huge oak tree next to a house on the left. From there, it's a straight shot across the river back to The Oaks Shopping Center.

Mile-by-Mile Directions	Distance to Next Turn	Total Distance
From The Oaks Shopping Center, turn LEFT on Shallowford Road (SR 1001), which becomes Courtney-Huntsville Road but remains SR 1001 when you cross the Yadkin River. Continue on SR 1001 to the stop sign at U.S. 601.	14.8	14.8
CROSS U.S. 601 on SR. 1001. The road name changes to Fish Brandon Road (SR 1165). Continue on Fish Brandon Road to the stop sign at Lone Hickory Road (SR 1002).	1.8	16.6
Turn LEFT on Lone Hickory Road and go to Joyner Road (SR 1156),	4.2	20.8
Turn LEFT on Joyner Road. The road number changes to SR 2106 when you enter Davie County. Continue on SR 2106 to the stop sign at Sandy Springs Road (SR 2105). The road sign is missing at this intersection.	1.9	22.7
Turn RIGHT on Sandy Springs Road and ride to Doby Road (SR 2111).	1.4	24.1
Turn LEFT on Doby Road and travel to the stop sign at Liberty Church Road (SR 1159).	3.3	27.4
Turn RIGHT on Liberty Church Road and go to Bell Branch Road (SR 1327).	0.5	27.9

Mile-by-Mile Directions	Distance to Next Turn	Total Distance
Turn LEFT on Bell Branch Road and ride to Chinquapin Road (SR 1164).	1.5	29.4
Go STRAIGHT on Chinquapin Road to the stop sign at Fish Brandon Road.	1.2	30.6
Turn RIGHT on Fish Brandon Road and ride to the stop sign at U.S. 601.	0.2	30.8
CROSS U.S. 601 onto Courtney-Huntsville/Shallowford Road and go to The Oaks Shopping Center on the right.	14.8	45.6

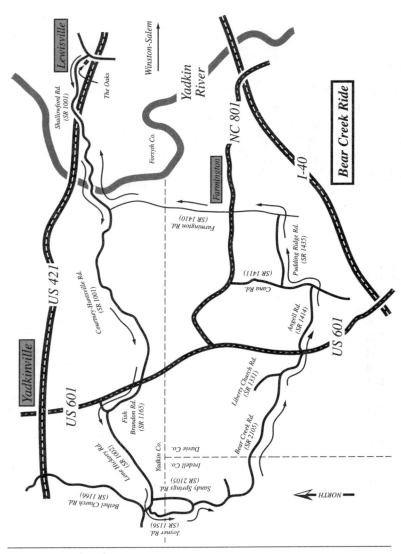

Bear Creek Ride

Description of the route

Cycling this route will reinforce the notion that most country roads in North Carolina are named either for people or churches. An exception is Monkey Bottom Road at the 10-mile mark as you ride out Shallowford/Courtney-Huntsville Road to the intersection with U.S. 601. Before you reach that intersection, you will see a well-preserved, historic brick house in front of what appears to be a partially underground house. However, the orientation to the west doesn't jibe with the standard notions of solar heating and insulation.

After riding 7.9 miles, you'll see a sign for the Dennis Popcorn Store, which is open Monday through Friday from 9:00 A.M. to 5:00 P.M. This 100+-acre farm boasts a plantation home for the Dennis family, who grows their own popcorn to supply their business. They sell bags of delicious, already-popped popcorn that's popular for parties and concession stands.

When you cross U.S. 601, the road name changes again to Fish Brandon Road. Some cyclists also call it "Stinky Farm Road." Just past Brawley Road, small goats frequently graze on the left. Down the road 1.1 miles on the right is Courtney Grocery. About 4 miles farther, N.C. Bike Route 2 turns

Starting point
  The Oaks Shopping Center in Lewisville
Distance
  50.1 miles
Terrain
  Rolling, with some good hills
Food and drinks
  The Oaks Shopping Center; Dennis Popcorn Store; Courtney Grocery; Gunter's Country Store
Recommendations
  Get in shape first.

left on Sandy Springs Road. In case you're wondering, Joyner Road was chosen to connect with Sandy Springs Road because it is flatter. The beginning of Sandy Springs Road has huge hills and a bad curve.

About 0.6 mile after the turn onto Joyner Road, the route crosses into Iredell County. The usual road surface has larger-than-normal pebbles in the tar. Judging from its narrow width, this may have been an old concrete road that's been paved over. Two miles after the turn onto Sandy Springs Road, you'll see Gunter's Country Store—a great place for a rest stop. The store is also open on Sunday mornings. The Turkeyfoot Country Market is 0.8 mile beyond. Somewhere along here the road name changes to Bear Creek—hence the route name. You'll see Bear Creek Baptist Church on your left.

Huge white pines brush the sky after you turn onto Liberty Church Road. Cana School, which operated from 1929 to 1941, offers architectural interest on your left at the intersection with Cana Road. The old Cana post office is on the right, before you cross Dutchman's Creek. Welcome to the hills on Pudding Ridge Road. Watch out for milk trucks serving the dairy farms on this road. Just before Cedar Creek Road, Pudding Ridge Golf Course is on the right. Farmington Road leads back to Courtney-Huntsville Road and on to Lewisville.

Mile-by-Mile Directions	Distance to Next Turn	Total Distance
From The Oaks Shopping Center, turn LEFT on Shallowford Road (SR 1001), which becomes Courtney-Huntsville Road but remains SR 1001 after you cross the Yadkin River. Continue on SR 1001 to the stop sign at U.S. 601.	14.4	14.4
CROSS U.S. 601 on Fish Brandon Road (SR 1165) and ride to Lone Hickory Road (SR 1002). You will see Renegar's Store (formerly Martin's Store) at this intersection.	1.8	16.2

Mile-by-Mile Directions	Distance to Next Turn	Total Distance
Turn LEFT on Lone Hickory Road and go to Joyner Road (SR 1156).	4.2	20.4
Turn LEFT on Joyner Road and continue to the stop sign at Sandy Springs Road (SR 2105).	2.0	22.4
Turn RIGHT on Sandy Springs Road, which becomes Bear Creek Road, and go to Liberty Church Road (SR 1159).	7.1	29.5
Turn RIGHT on Liberty Church Road and go to the unnamed road on the left at the stop sign.	1.0	30.5
Turn LEFT on the unnamed road and ride to the stop sign at U.S. 601.	0.1	30.6
CROSS U.S. 601 on Angell Road and go to the stop sign at Cana Road (SR 1411).	2.6	33.2
Turn LEFT on Cana Road and continue to Pudding Ridge Road (SR 1435).	1.2	34.4
Turn RIGHT on Pudding Ridge Road and go to the stop sign at Farmington Road (SR 1410).	2.6	37.0
Turn LEFT on Farmington Road and continue to the stop sign at N.C. 801.	1.9	38.9
CROSS N.C. 801 on Farmington Road, which becomes SR 1716 (the road number changes after you cross N.C. 801), and go to the stop sign at Courtney-Huntsville/Shallowford Road (SR 1001).	4.6	43.5
Turn RIGHT on Courtney-Huntsville/Shallowford Road and ride to The Oaks Shopping Center on the right.	6.6	50.1

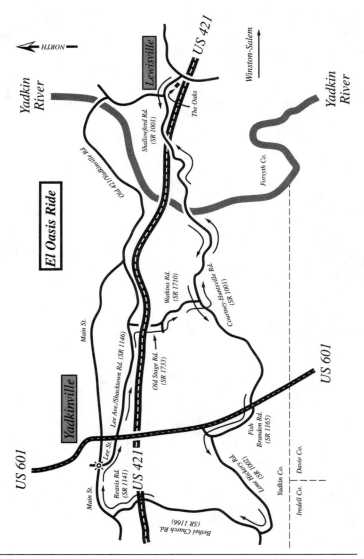

El Oasis Ride

Description of the route

A sign in front of a local church on this route once read: "We may not be Dairy Queen, but we have great Sundays." This serves as a reminder that part of the joy of bicycling is seeing interesting and unusual things along the way.

After you survive the curvy climb on Lone Hickory Road to Bethel Church Road, this route provides some great views of the mountains. Just after the turn, you'll marvel at the great views of both Pilot Knob and Sauratown Mountain. Barely a tenth of a mile later, you'll add a view of Hanging Rock. As you pedal through the open farmland, you can also see the Brushy Mountains to your left. That's quite an unusual line-up of views. A nice downhill flattens out at the bottom as you move past a large farm with major silos before starting your climb.

At this writing, construction on U.S. 421 surrounds Bethel Church Road, but a new overpass should soon carry cyclists over the busy four-lane highway. This will be a safer and more pleasant change from crossing the highway at grade. After you cross U.S. 421,

Starting point
  The Oaks Shopping Center in Lewisville
Distance
  45.3 miles
Terrain
  Rolling, with a few hills
Food and drinks
  The Oaks Shopping Center, Yadkinville
Recommendations
  Have your climbing legs ready.

the road name changes to Reavis Road. There's a beautiful shot of the Brushy Mountains just before the stop sign at Main Street/Old 421. After you turn onto Main Street and travel 0.8 mile into Yadkinville, you'll see El Oasis convenience store on the right. This is the spot that inspired the name for this ride. About 1.7 miles later, you'll pass Harmony Heights Animal Hospital and one of the best road names in the area—Booger Swamp Road.

Mile-by-Mile Directions	Distance to Next Turn	Total Distance
From The Oaks Shopping Center, turn LEFT on Shallowford Road (SR 1001), which becomes Courtney-Huntsville Road but remains SR 1001 when it crosses the Yadkin River. Continue on SR 1001 to the stop sign at U.S. 601.	14.4	14.4
CROSS U.S. 601 onto Fish Brandon Road (SR 1165) and ride to Lone Hickory Road (SR 1002).	1.8	16.2
Turn LEFT on Lone Hickory Road and continue to Bethel Church Road (SR 1166).	4.4	20.6
Turn RIGHT on Bethel Church Road and go to the stop sign at U.S. 421.	4.1	24.7
CROSS U.S. 421 on Reavis Road (SR 1141) and ride to the stop sign at Old 421 (SR 1314).	1.2	25.9
Turn RIGHT on Old 421, which becomes Main Street in Yadkinville. Continue on Main Street to North Lee Avenue.	2.1	28.0
Turn RIGHT on North Lee Street and go to South State Street.	1.2	29.2

Mile-by-Mile Directions	Distance to Next Turn	Total Distance
CROSS South State Street at the stop sign onto East Lee Avenue, which becomes Shacktown Road (SR 1146). Continue on Shacktown Road to Old Stage Road (SR 1733).	4.2	33.4
Turn RIGHT on Old Stage Road and pass under U.S. 421 to Watkins Road (SR 1710).	0.8	34.2
Turn LEFT on Watkins Road and ride to Courtney-Huntsville Road NOTE: There is a hard left turn in a blind curve.	1.7	35.9
Turn LEFT on Courtney-Huntsville/ Shallowford Road and go to The Oaks Shopping Center on the right.	9.4	45.3

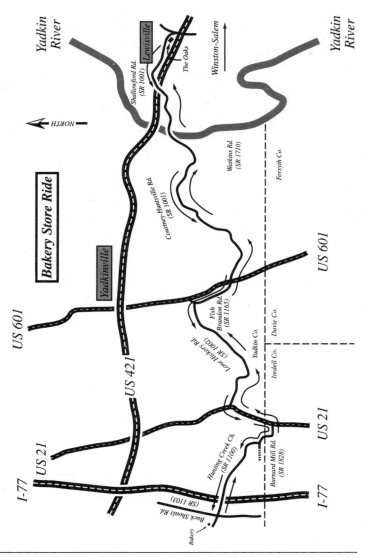

Bakery Store Ride

You'll hardly believe you're still in North Carolina on this ride to the Amish community of Windsor Crossroads. It's surprising that you can go this distance with so few turns and so few hills: you ride 14 miles before the first turn! After 7.8 miles, you'll see the

Starting point
The Oaks Shopping Center in Lewisville

Distance
58.1 miles

Terrain
Surprisingly level, except for a few hills

Food and drinks
The Oaks Shopping Center; Courtney Grocery; Goder's Community Market; Dennis Popcorn Store

Recommendations
Take plenty of money to chow down at the bakery.

sign for the Dennis Popcorn Store, located down a road on the right. The store is open Monday through Friday from 9:00 A.M. to 5:00 P.M. After you climb the big hill up from the Yadkin River, this section is flat to rolling.

There's a slight climb after you pass Dinkins Bottom Road. The houses are close to the road in this section. Supposedly, the community of Huntsville was two votes shy of being voted the capital of North Carolina. Evidently, it was a thriving town before the Civil War. At mile 13.2, you'll pass the Courtney Grocery. When you see a sign for N.C. Bike Route 2, you'll also see some vineyards. Lone Hickory Road provides gorgeous views of the mountains to the right and straight ahead. Once on U.S. 21, you enter Iredell County. After 1.2 miles, you'll see The Rabbit Bar on the left.

Along Barnard Mill Road, you cross a beautiful stream at the bottom of the hill, followed by a sweeping expanse of pastureland on the right. At the turn onto Hunting Creek Church Road, there's no road sign but there is a sign for Hunting Creek Friends Meeting. After passing over I-77, you'll see the lovely brick chapel on the right. After crossing Buck Shoals Road, you enter the Amish community of Windsor Crossroads. You'll see a very old plank house with a leaning tower and other outbuildings on your right. The Amish bakery is housed in Goder's Community Market, a one-story white building on the right. Although closed on Sunday and Monday, it is open Tuesday through Saturday from 8:00 A.M. to 6:00 P.M.

Mile-by-Mile Directions	Distance to Next Turn	Total Distance
From The Oaks Shopping Center, turn LEFT on Shallowford Road (SR 1001), which becomes Courtney-Huntsville Road but remains SR 1001 after crossing the Yadkin River. Continue on SR 1001 to the stop sign at U.S. 601.	14.3	14.3
CROSS U.S. 601, where Courtney-Huntsville Road changes to Fish Brandon Road (SR 1165). Continue on Fish Brandon Road to Lone Hickory Road (SR 1002).	1.8	16.1
Turn LEFT on Lone Hickory Road and ride to the stop sign at U.S. 21.	5.7	21.8

Mile-by-Mile Directions	Distance to Next Turn	Total Distance
Turn LEFT on U.S. 21 and go to Barnard Mill Road (SR 1828).	1.7	23.5
Turn RIGHT on Barnard Mill Road and ride to Hunting Creek Church Road (SR 1100), which appears just before the pavement ends.	1.3	24.8
Turn RIGHT on Hunting Creek Road and go to the stop sign at Buck Shoals Road (SR 1103).	3.3	28.1
CROSS Buck Shoals Road, where Hunting Creek Church Road becomes Windsor Road. Continue on Windsor Road to Yoder's Community Market.	0.9	29.0
Turn LEFT on Windsor Road and ride to the stop sign at Buck Shoals Road.	0.9	29.9
CROSS Buck Shoals Road onto Hunting Creek Church Road and continue to the stop sign at Barnard Mill Road.	3.3	33.2
Turn LEFT on Barnard Mill Road and ride to the stop sign at U.S. 21.	1.3	34.51.7
Turn LEFT on U.S. 21 and go to Lone Hickory Road.	36.2	
Turn RIGHT on Lone Hickory Road and ride to the stop sign at Fish Brandon Road.	5.7	41.9
Turn RIGHT on Fish Brandon Road and continue to the stop sign at U.S. 601.	1.8	43.7
CROSS U.S. 601 onto Courtney-Huntsville/Shallowford Road and travel to The Oaks Shopping Center on the right.	14.4	58.1

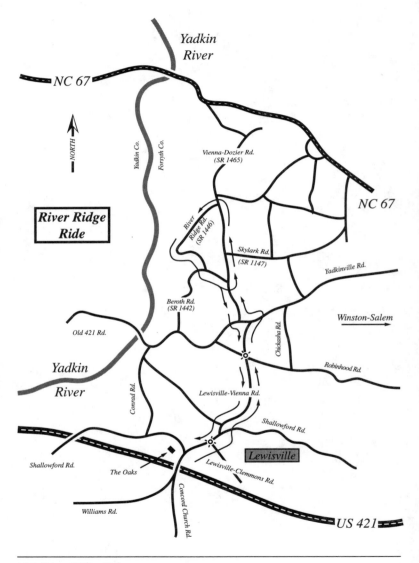

River Ridge Ride

NORTH

Yadkin River

NC 67

Yadkin Co.

Forsyth Co.

Vienna-Dozier Rd.
(SR 1465)

NC 67

River Ridge Rd.
(SR 1446)

Skylark Rd.
(SR 1147)

Yadkinville Rd.

Beroth Rd.
(SR 1442)

Winston-Salem

Old 421 Rd.

Chickasha Rd.

Robinhood Rd.

Yadkin River

Conrad Rd.

Lewisville-Vienna Rd.

Shallowford Rd.

Lewisville

Shallowford Rd.

The Oaks

Lewisville-Clemmons Rd.

Williams Rd.

Concord Church Rd.

US 421

River Ridge Ride

Like many of the rides in this book, this route starts at The Oaks Shopping Center. From The Oaks, you will first travel on Shallowford Road, which is the main street through downtown Lewisville.

This route makes a good training ride because you have the option of circling the River Ridge/Vienna-Dozier Loop as many times as you wish to add mileage. If time is short, you can do one quick loop after work. Shallowford and Lewisville-Vienna Roads connect with area housing developments, so they have a certain amount of traffic all the time. The traffic increases during morning and evening rush hours. You'll want to take the traffic into account when planning your ride.

Lewisville-Vienna Road is a pleasant, fairly level portion of the route that travels through a more established residential area of Lewisville. The route gives way to newer homes farther out. Yadkinville Road can be very busy, but fortunately you're on this road for a short distance. Vienna-Dozier Road retains its country atmosphere, with large green areas and widely spaced houses. River Ridge Road winds past large homes interspersed with cornfields and woods as though it can't decide whether it's town or

Starting point
   The Oaks Shopping Center in Lewisville
Distance
   13.4 miles, with the option for more loops
Terrain
   Rolling, with some good hills
Food and drinks
   The Oaks Shopping Center
Recommendations
   This is a very good training ride.

country. The traffic is light along River Ridge Road, so it's a good place to expand your riding distance by making a loop that circles from River Ridge Road to Vienna-Dozier Road and back to River Ridge Road.

Mile-by-Mile Directions	Distance to Next Turn	Total Distance
From The Oaks Shopping Center, turn RIGHT on Shallowford Road and travel to the stop sign at the intersection with Williams Road (SR 1173).	0.1	0.1
Turn LEFT on Shallowford Road and ride to Lewisville-Vienna Road (SR 1308).	0.8	0.9
Turn LEFT on Lewisville-Vienna Road and go to the signal at Robinhood Road.	2.1	3.0
CROSS Robinhood Road and go to the stop sign at Yadkinville Road (SR 1561).	0.9	3.9
Turn LEFT on Yadkinville Road and go to Vienna-Dozier Road (SR 1465).	0.6	4.5
Turn RIGHT on Vienna-Dozier Road and ride to River Ridge Road (SR 1446).	0.7	5.2
Turn LEFT on River Ridge Road and go to the stop sign at Vienna-Dozier Road.	3.1	8.3
Turn RIGHT on Vienna-Dozier Road and go to the stop sign at Yadkinville Road.	0.7	9.0
Turn LEFT on Yadkinville Road and ride to Lewisville-Vienna Road.	0.6	9.6
Turn RIGHT on Lewisville-Vienna Road and travel to the stop sign at Shallowford Road.	3.0	12.6
Turn RIGHT on Shallowford Road and ride to The Oaks Shopping Center, which will be on your right.	0.8	13.4

Randy Shields' Training Ride

Description of the route

Randy Shields volunteered this route, which is one of his favorite training rides. The entire route is located in Forsyth County. From The Oaks Shopping Center, you will travel to Lewisville-Vienna Road, which has a fair amount of traffic. Fortunately, the speed limit is only 45 miles per hour. Robinhood and Yadkinville Roads are major thoroughfares in Winston-Salem and can be very busy, but the distance you travel on both these roads is short.

Although the county roads on this ride are not truly rural, the houses are spaced far apart and the traffic is light. The rolling countryside offers some interesting ups and downs. You'll see a pretty, little brick church on Seward Road. Then Kilmurry Hill Road wends its way through woods, past horses grazing lazily, oblivious to spinning pedals.

Starting point
The Oaks Shopping Center in Lewisville
Distance
23.0 miles
Terrain
Rolling
Food and drinks
The Oaks Shopping Center
Recommendations
This is a good training ride.

The return route offers some different scenery on Vienna-Dozier and River Ridge Roads. Vienna and Dozier are small communities in this area. River Ridge is lined intermittently with large homes and the remnants of what were once large farms. When you get to Yadkinville and later Lewisville-Vienna Roads, you'll have to make the transition back to traffic and people in a hurry.

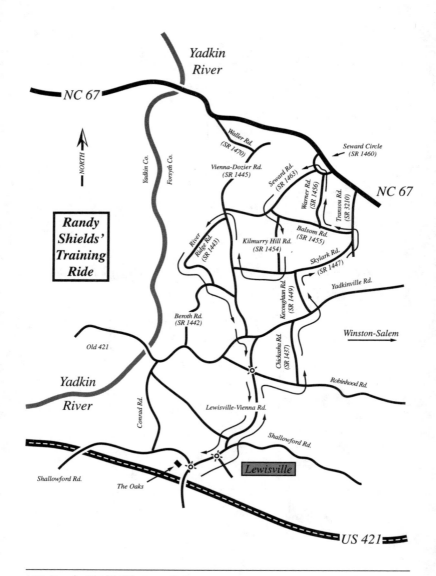

Randy Shields' Training Ride

Mile-by-Mile Directions	Distance to Next Turn	Total Distance
From The Oaks Shopping Center, turn LEFT on Shallowford Road (SR 1001) and travel to Lewisville-Vienna Road (SR 1308).	0.8	0.8
Turn LEFT on Lewisville-Vienna Road and go to the signal at Robinhood Road.	2.1	2.9
Turn RIGHT on Robinhood Road and ride to Chickasha Road (SR 1437).	0.9	3.8
Turn LEFT on Chickasha Road and go to the stop sign at Yadkinville Road (SR 1561).	1.5	5.3
Turn RIGHT on Yadkinville Road and go to Kecoughtan Road (SR 1449).	0.4	5.7
Turn LEFT on Kecoughtan Road and go to the stop sign at Skylark Road (SR 1447).	0.7	6.4
Turn RIGHT on Skylark Road and ride to the stop sign at Transou Road (SR 3210).	1.6	8.0
Turn LEFT on Transou Road and travel 50 feet before turning LEFT on Balsom Road (SR 1455). Stay on Balsom Road to Warner Road (SR 1456).	0.6	8.6
Turn RIGHT on Warner Road and ride to the stop sign at Seward Circle (SR 1460).	1.2	9.8

Mile-by-Mile Directions	Distance to Next Turn	Total Distance
Turn LEFT on Seward Circle and travel to Seward Road (SR 1463).	0.3	10.1
Turn LEFT on Seward Road and go to Balsom Road again.	1.6	11.7
Turn LEFT on Balsom Road and ride to Kilmurry Hill Road (SR 1454).	0.2	11.9
Turn RIGHT on Kilmurry Hill Road and go to Skylark Road again.	1.4	13.3
Turn RIGHT on Skylark Road and go to Vienna-Dozier Road (SR 1465).	1.0	14.3
Turn RIGHT on Vienna-Dozier Road and ride to River Ridge Road (SR 1443).	1.1	15.4
Turn LEFT on River Ridge and travel to the stop sign at Yadkinville Road.	3.5	18.9
Turn LEFT on Yadkinville Road and go to Lewisville-Vienna Road again.	0.2	19.1
Turn RIGHT on Lewisville-Vienna Road and ride to the stop sign at Shallowford Road.	3.1	22.2
Turn RIGHT on Shallowford Road and travel through the traffic signal at Lewisville-Clemmons Road. After the traffic signal, turn RIGHT and travel to The Oaks Shopping Center.	0.8	23.0

Tobaccoville All Hills Ride

Description of the route

Don't be fooled by the pleasant rolling terrain at the beginning of this ride. Most of the hills come at the end of the ride, so save some energy. The first part of the ride passes through residential areas—first in Lewisville, then in Old Town. The houses are spread farther

Starting point
The Oaks Shopping Center in Lewisville

Distance
33.2 miles

Terrain
Rolling, then quite hilly

Food and drinks
The Oaks Shopping Center; East Bend; an occasional country store

Recommendations
Try to avoid N.C. 67 during peak traffic hours

apart when you get to Kilmurry Hill Road. This curvy road traverses woods, then passes verdant pastures where horses graze lazily.

On Seward Road, a pretty little brick church graces the road on the left. N.C. 67 can be quite busy with traffic, so take care. Fortunately, your travel on this main road is short. After you turn onto Tobaccoville Road, you'll see Old

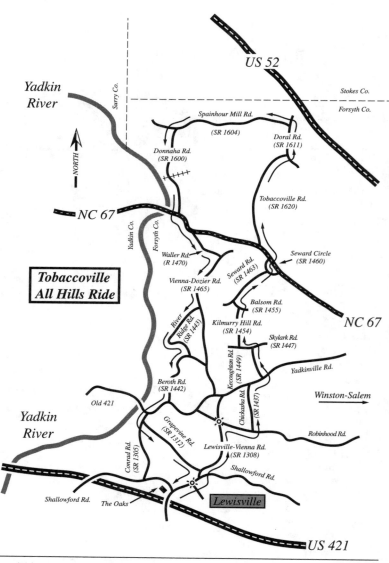

Yadkin
River

US 52

Stokes Co.

Surry Co.

Forsyth Co.

NORTH

Spainhour Mill Rd.
(SR 1604)

Doral Rd.
(SR 1611)

Donnaha Rd.
(SR 1600)

— NC 67

Tobaccoville Rd.
(SR 1620)

Yadkin Co.

Forsyth Co.

Waller Rd.
(R 1470)

Seward Circle
(SR 1460)

**Tobaccoville
All Hills Ride**

Vienna-Dozier Rd.
(SR 1465)

Seward Rd.
(SR 1463)

Balsom Rd.
(SR 1455)

River
Ridge Rd.
(SR 1443)

Kilmurry Hill Rd.
(SR 1454)

Skylark Rd.
(SR 1447)

NC 67

Kecoughtan Rd. (SR 1449)

Yadkinville Rd.

Beroth Rd.
(SR 1442)

Chickasha Rd. (SR 1437)

Winston-Salem

Old 421

Grapevine Rd.
(SR 1312)

Robinhood Rd.

Yadkin
River

Conrad Rd.
(SR 1305)

Lewisville-Vienna Rd.
(SR 1308)

Shallowford Rd.

Shallowford Rd.

The Oaks

Lewisville

US 421

Richmond School on the left. The flashing light at the intersection of Tobaccoville and Doral Roads marks the heart of the small town of Tobaccoville. You'll see the town hall on your left. Doral Road is the main thoroughfare through town and has a lot of traffic, although the speed limit is only 35 miles per hour. Spainhour Mill Road can also have quite a bit of traffic.

Donnaha Road is mainly level, because it parallels the river. Watch out for the bad railroad tracks at the King water plant. The next stretch of N.C. 67 provides a challenging hill, but it does have a narrow shoulder for a little breathing room. On Vienna-Dozier Road, be sure to bear left in front of Waller's Grocery. As you do, look for an interesting house with a lovely lake on the left. River Ridge Road takes you past large homes, interspersed with cornfields and woods. Grapevine Road and its big climb is the final challenge as you re-enter Lewisville and the end of the ride.

Mile-by-Mile Directions	Distance to Next Turn	Total Distance
From The Oaks Shopping Center, turn LEFT on Shallowford Road (SR 1001), which is the main street through downtown Lewisville. Continue to Lewisville-Vienna Road (SR 1308).	0.8	0.8
Turn LEFT on Lewisville-Vienna Road and ride to the signal at Robinhood Road.	2.1	2.9
Turn RIGHT on Robinhood Road and go to Chickasha Road (SR 1437).	0.9	3.8
Turn LEFT on Chickasha Road and ride to the stop sign at Yadkinville Road (SR 1561).	1.5	5.3
Turn RIGHT on Yadkinville Road and travel to Kecoughtan Road (SR 1449).	0.4	5.7
Turn LEFT on Kecoughtan Road and continue to the stop sign at Skylark Road (SR 1447).	0.7	6.4

Mile-by-Mile Directions	Distance to Next Turn	Total Distance
Turn LEFT on Skylark Road and go to Kilmurry Hill Road (SR 1454).	0.3	6.7
Turn RIGHT on Kilmurry Hill Road and ride to Balsom Road (SR 1455).	1.5	8.2
Turn LEFT on Balsom Road and go to the stop sign at Seward Road (SR 1463).	1.6	9.8
Turn RIGHT on Seward Road and ride to Seward Circle (SR 1460).	0.1	9.9
Turn LEFT on Seward Circle and travel to N.C. 67.	0.8	10.7
Turn LEFT on N.C. 67 and continue to Tobaccoville Road (SR 1620).	1.0	11.7
Turn RIGHT on Tobaccoville Road, then bear immediately to the LEFT. Continue to the flashing light at Doral Road (SR 1611) and ride into the town of Tobaccoville.	3.0	14.7
Turn LEFT on Doral Road and travel to Spainhour Mill Road (SR 1604).	3.6	18.3
Turn LEFT on Spainhour Mill Road and ride to Donnaha Road (SR 1600).	2.5	20.8
Turn LEFT on Donnaha Road and continue to the stop sign at N.C. 67.	0.9	21.7
Turn LEFT on N.C. 67 and ride to Waller Road (SR 1470).	1.4	23.1
Turn RIGHT on Waller Road and go to the stop sign at Vienna-Dozier Road (SR 1465).	1.9	25.0
Turn RIGHT on Vienna-Dozier Road and travel to River Ridge Road (SR 1443).	2.3	27.3

Mile-by-Mile Directions	Distance to Next Turn	Total Distance
Turn RIGHT on River Ridge Road and go to Beroth Road (SR 1442).	1.6	28.9
Turn RIGHT on Beroth Road and continue to the stop sign at Yadkinville Road.	0.7	29.6
Turn RIGHT on Yadkinville Road. Yadkinville Road will bear to the right when it forks with Conrad Road (SR 1305). Continue on Conrad Road to Grapevine Road (SR 1312).	0.4	30.0
Turn LEFT on Grapevine Road and travel to Lewisville-Vienna Road.	0.1	30.1
Turn RIGHT on Lewisville-Vienna Road and ride to the stop sign at Shallowford Road.	2.3	32.4
Turn RIGHT on Shallowford Road and go through the traffic signal at Lewisville-Clemmons Road. Turn RIGHT into The Oaks Shopping Center.	0.8	33.2

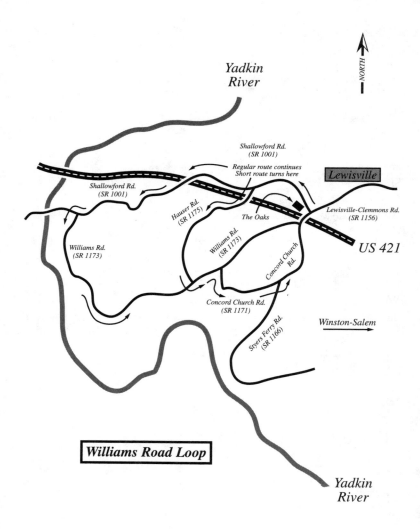

Yadkin
River

NORTH

Shallowford Rd.
(SR 1001)

Regular route continues
Short route turns here

Lewisville

Shallowford Rd.
(SR 1001)

Hauser Rd.
(SR 1175)

The Oaks

Lewisville-Clemmons Rd.
(SR 1156)

Williams Rd.
(SR 1173)

US 421

Williams Rd.
(SR 1173)

Concord Church
Rd.

Concord Church Rd.
(SR 1171)

Winston-Salem

Styers Ferry Rd.
(SR 1166)

Williams Road Loop

Yadkin
River

Williams Road Loop

This loop is a favorite training ride because the scenery is so pretty, and there's little traffic except on the first stretch of Shallowford Road. Shallowford Road leads to one of the shallowest points on the Yadkin River—hence the road's name. This part of Forsyth County is known as West Bend because the Yadkin River forms a shape like a crone's nose as it turns west, making one of the most distinctive shapes on the Forsyth County map.

The fertile, sunny fields in this area convinced the Kroustalis family to purchase land and plant the grape varietals that were the beginning of Westbend Vineyards. After several years of tender care, the vineyards produced sufficient grapes for the winemaker to make Westbend wines. The wines have won both regional and national awards for their quality and distinctive flavor. So much for the naysayers who maintained that the red clay of Piedmont North Carolina was not good for producing wines!

Once you turn left onto Williams Road, you'll see the vineyards ahead on both sides of the road. In summer, you can see the clusters of immature grapes. At harvest time during

Starting point
The Oaks Shopping Center in Lewisville
Distance
12.9 miles
Terrain
Rolling, with some hills
Food and drinks
The Oaks Shopping Center
Recommendations
This is a great ride almost any time.

August and September, you'll see workers who cut the clusters, drop them into special carts, and take them to the winery.

Williams Road has very little traffic. It is woodsy in some places and humid in others. When in the woods, enjoy the break before you head back into the sun and the ups and downs that lead you back into Lewisville. Concord Church and Williams Roads are quite busy around U.S. 421 and going into Lewisville, but most drivers are courteous.

Mile-by-Mile Directions	Distance to Next Turn	Total Distance
From The Oaks Shopping Center, turn LEFT on Shallowford Road, traveling away from Lewisville towards Williams Road (SR 1173).	4.8	4.8
Turn LEFT on Williams Road and ride to Concord Church Road (SR 1171).	4.9	9.7
Turn RIGHT on Concord Church Road and go to the stop sign at the intersection with Styers Ferry Road (SR 1166).	1.5	11.2
Turn LEFT on Concord Church Road. Styers Ferry Road, which goes to the right, actually begins here. Concord Church Road's name changes to Williams Road at the intersection with U.S. 421. Continue on Williams Road to The Oaks Shopping Center on the left.	1.7	12.9

OPTION: For a shorter loop, after 1.3 miles, you can turn LEFT off Shallowford onto Hauser Road. Hauser Road will take you to Williams Road, then on to Concord Church Road, where you can pick up the rest of this route.

Thursday Night Training Ride

Description of the route

After leaving The Oaks Shopping Center, there are few turns on this ride, although the road names change as the road you're on turns off the main road. For example, Williams Road goes off to the right just past the U.S. 421 bridge. Concord Church Road begins here and then goes off to the right just past Dull Road. On this loop, the houses are spaced far apart. You will also pass horse farms and lush pastures before enjoying the thrilling downhill on Dull Road that leads to the creek. But, watch out. You have to climb the other side of the hill. After topping the hill, there's an interesting log house on the left, if you're not too stressed to enjoy it.

The Citgo station on the corner of Dull and Styers Ferry Roads offers convenience-store food and drinks. Just past the station on the right is a lovely sheep farm with a stone house. If you didn't know better, you'd think you were in Scotland. The family who lives there produces wool from their sheep.

Starting point
The Oaks Shopping Center in Lewisville

Distance
8.4 miles

Terrain
Rolling to hilly

Food and drinks
The Oaks Shopping Center; Citgo Station at the corner of Dull Road and Styers Ferry Road

Recommendations
This is a great ride for evenings after work.

Styers Ferry Road then makes a grand sweep through an upscale housing development before sailing downhill and across a small stream. You can see more horses on this part of the route. Fortunately, there's usually not much traffic on this section of the route. On your way back to Lewisville, you'll pass Willow Run Club, nestled in the woods on your right. The route then passes through the Runnymede development. Stables and another horse farm sit on your right just after you pass Dull Road.

Mile-by-Mile Directions	Distance to Next Turn	Total Distance
From The Oaks Shopping Center, turn RIGHT on Williams Road (SR 1173) and CROSS U.S. 421 to Dull Road (SR 1170).	1.1	1.1
Turn LEFT on Dull Road and travel to the stop sign at Styers Ferry Road (SR 1100).	1.1	2.2
Turn RIGHT on Styers Ferry Road (SR 1100) to a point where Styers Ferry Road turns to the right.	0.5	2.7
Follow Styers Ferry Road as it turns RIGHT. The name of the main road changes to Lasater Road at this location. Travel on Styers Ferry Road, which is now SR 1166, to Dull Road. The name of the road changes to Concord Church Road (SR 1171), right after you pass Falmouth Road.	4.6	7.3
CONTINUE straight on Concord Church Road, which then becomes Williams Road. Stay on Williams Road to The Oaks Shopping Center, which is on the left.	1.1	8.4

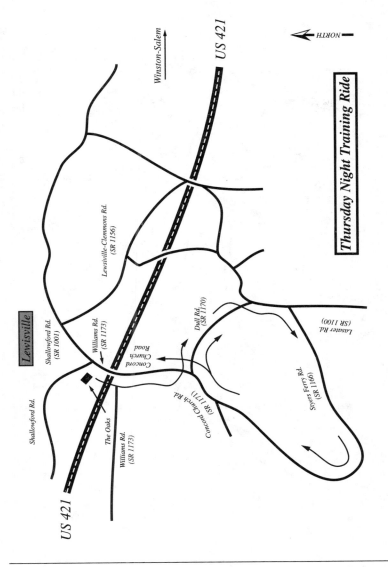

Lewisville

Shallowford Rd.
(SR 1001)

Williams Rd.
(SR 1173)

Shallowford Rd.

The Oaks

Williams Rd.
(SR 1173)

Concord
Church
Road

Concord Church Rd.
(SR 1171)

Dull Rd.
(SR 1170)

Lasater Rd.
(SR 1100)

Styers Ferry Rd.
(SR 1166)

Lewisville-Clemmons Rd.
(SR 1156)

Winston-Salem

US 421

US 421

NORTH

Thursday Night Training Ride

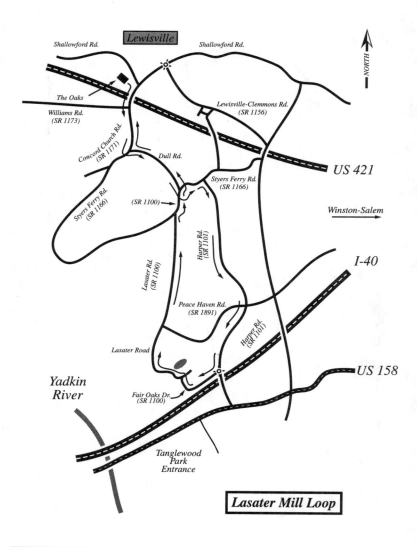

Lasater Mill Loop

Starting point
  The Oaks Shopping Center
  in Lewisville

Distance
  13.0 miles (There is an option
  for a shorter 8.6-mile loop.)

Terrain
  Rolling, with a couple of good
  climbs

Food and drinks
  The Oaks Shopping Center;
  the Citgo Station at the
  intersection of Dull and Styers
  Ferry Roads

Recommendations
  Take time to enjoy the mill
  and pond.

Description of the route

This short, but interesting, ride skirts the towns of Lewisville and Clemmons, passing through some lovely residential areas. Traffic is usually light but can be heavy at certain times of the day, especially on Styers Ferry Road.

After you turn from Harper Road onto Fair Oaks Drive,

Mile-by-Mile Directions	Distance to Next Turn	Total Distance
From The Oaks Shopping Center, turn RIGHT on Williams Road (SR 1173) and ride toward U.S. 421 to Dull Road (SR 1170).	1.1	1.1
Turn LEFT on Dull Road and travel to Styers Ferry Road (SR 1100).	1.1	2.2
Turn LEFT on Styers Ferry Road (SR 1166) and go to Harper Road (SR 1101).	0.4	2.6
Turn RIGHT on Harper Road and go to Peace Haven Road (SR 1891).	2.3	4.9
CROSS Peace Haven Road and travel to Fair Oaks Drive (SR 1100).	1.5	6.4
Turn RIGHT on Fair Oaks Drive and ride to the stop sign at Lasater Road, which is also SR 1100.	0.7	7.1
Turn LEFT on Lasater Road and go to Dull Road.	3.7	10.8
Turn RIGHT on Dull Road and ride to Concord Church Road (SR 1171).	1.1	11.9
Turn RIGHT on Concord Church Road. The road becomes Williams Road at the intersection with U.S. 421. Continue on Williams Road to The Oaks Shopping Center on the left.	1.1	13.0

Option: For an 8.6-mile version of this ride, you can start at the Citgo station on the corner of Dull and Styers Ferry Roads. This option also eliminates the two large hills on Dull Road.

you'll hear and sometimes see I-40 through the trees that screen the highway on the left. Once you turn onto Lasater Road, the Blumenthal Jewish Home is nestled back from the road among the trees on your left.

The most beautiful part of the route winds down shady Lasater Road and past the Lasater Mill and pond. The current owners have preserved the wonderful stone buildings and fence. They have also enhanced the surroundings with lovely plantings and landscaping. There are places to pull over on either side of the road, but take care because visibility is poor due to the curve in the road. The mill wheel still turns, and it's refreshing to stop on the right side of the road where you can watch the wheel and listen to water cascading from the millpond.

In return for this wonderful view, you then have to climb a gradual hill to complete the loop. But, it's well worth it. On this popular ride, you may well encounter other cyclists who've stopped to admire the view.

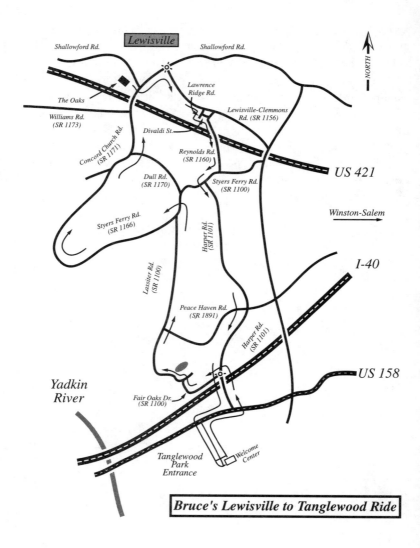

Bruce's Lewisville to Tanglewood Ride

Bruce's Lewisville to Tanglewood Ride

This route was named for Bruce Heye, a friend who happens to live in Lewisville just off this route.

This interesting route connects the towns of Lewisville and Clemmons to Tanglewood Park. A different return route from Tanglewood will keep you from getting bored with what you see. The ride starts from The Oaks Shopping Center, passes through Lewisville until you take a right turn at the traffic signal on Lewisville-Clemmons Road. This road is quite busy, so this tour takes a less-busy route through the neighborhoods to get to Harper Road, which is near Tanglewood Park.

Harper Road offers some ups and downs, with curves thrown in for good measure. It ends at U.S. 158, where a right turn leads

Starting point
The Oaks Shopping Center in Lewisville

Distance
18.2 miles (longer if you decide to ride inside Tanglewood Park)

Terrain
Rolling

Food and drinks
The Oaks Shopping Center; vending machines and concessions are available at Tanglewood during certain hours.

Recommendations
Avoid U.S. 158, Shallowford Road, and Lewisville-Clemmons Road during rush hours. Take a few dollars with you. The entrance fee at Tanglewood is $2 per car or bike.

to the Tanglewood entrance 0.4 mile away. U.S. 158 is a busy, five-lane highway, so take special care here. The center left-turn lane affords some protection. We recommend saving this ride for off-peak hours because of the heavy traffic during rush hours on some of these roads.

Tanglewood Park, a 1,300-acre recreation area, was originally the estate of Will Reynolds and his wife. Will was the brother of R.J. Reynolds, founder of Reynolds Tobacco Company. It's a wonderful place to explore by bike. The roads are narrow lanes with lots of hills and sweeping curves, but the speed limit is low. The park facilities include two golf courses, a par-3 course, stables, a swimming pool, tennis courts, campgrounds, paddleboard and canoe rentals, and picnic areas scattered throughout the park. We encourage you to explore all the different roads. If you're a mountain biker, you may also want to ride the mountain-bike trails here. (See the "Mountain Bike Trails" section.)

The return starts with Harper Road but turns onto Fair Oaks Drive on the other side of the I-40 bridge. From Fair Oaks Drive, you take Lasater Road, which curves downhill to a lovely stone mill and pond that have been wonderfully restored. After your climb to the more level section of Lasater Road, you'll pass the huge new Center Grove Church on your left. Styers Ferry Road, which has light traffic, takes you past horse farms as you pedal back to Lewisville and The Oaks Shopping Center.

Mile-by-Mile Directions	Distance to Next Turn	Total Distance
From The Oaks Shopping Center, turn LEFT on the east-west portion of Shallowford Road and go to Lewisville-Clemmons Road (SR 1156).	0.5	0.5
Turn RIGHT on Lewisville-Clemmons Road and ride to Lawrence Ridge Road.	0.7	1.2
Turn RIGHT on Lawrence Ridge Road and go to Divaldi Street.	0.1	1.3

Mile-by-Mile Directions	Distance to Next Turn	Total Distance
Turn LEFT on Divaldi Street and ride to Reynolds Road (SR 1160).	0.3	1.6
Turn RIGHT on Reynolds Road and travel to Styers Ferry Road (SR 1100).	0.9	2.5
Turn RIGHT on Styers Ferry Road and go to Harper Road (SR 1101).	0.3	2.8
Turn LEFT on Harper Road and travel to Peace Haven Road (SR 1891).	2.3	5.1
CROSS Peace Haven Road and ride to U.S. 158.	1.7	6.8
Turn RIGHT on U.S. 158 and go to the entrance to Tanglewood Park.	0.4	7.2
Turn LEFT into Tanglewood Park and go to the first intersection. The welcome center, where you can pick up maps if its open, will be on your left.	0.2	7.4
Although there are several options for biking inside the park, one recommended ride is to continue straight on Tanglewood Drive, past the stable, the manor house, tennis courts, and swimming pool. Turn RIGHT at the train and ride past the barn, Skilpot Lake and the BMX track. This road will loop back into Tanglewood Drive, where you will turn LEFT and return to the main entrance. If you want to mountain bike, see the Tanglewood trails under "Mountain Bike Trails." Because you may choose other options, the mileage listed below is measured only from the welcome center to the park entrance.	0.2	7.6
Turn RIGHT on U.S. 158 to Harper Road.	0.4	8.0

Mile-by-Mile Directions	Distance to Next Turn	Total Distance
Turn LEFT on Harper Road and go to Fair Oaks Drive (SR 1100).	0.3	8.3
Turn LEFT on Fair Oaks Drive and ride to Lasater Road (SR 1100).	0.8	9.1
Turn LEFT on Lasater Road and go to Styers Ferry Road (SR 1166).	3.2	12.3
Turn LEFT on Styers Ferry Road and go to Concord Church Road. Concord Church Road becomes Williams Road after crossing U.S. 421. Continue on Williams Road to The Oaks Shopping Center on the left.	5.9	18.2

Lower Yadkin Loop

This route begins in two of Forsyth County's smaller towns and wends its way toward the Yadkin River. The first couple of miles travel through residential sections of Clemmons and along Clemmons's main business area, which is south of I-40. Once you turn onto Hampton Road, the residential area changes to farmland. The farms grow bigger and more beautiful the closer you get to the river. Hampton Road is flat or downhill for over 6 miles as it travels to Muddy Creek. The road then climbs past the spacious farm and grand house of Richard Childress, the NASCAR race-car owner.

Starting point
The Oaks Shopping Center in Lewisville

Distance
52.7 miles

Terrain
Rolling hills

Food and drinks
The Oaks Shopping Center; stores along Lewisville-Clemmons Road; the store at the intersection of N.C. 801 and Farmington Road.

Recommendations
This ride is best on the weekend because of traffic along Lewisville-Clemmons Road and U.S. 64.

U.S. 64 is the route of necessity because it's the only way across the Yadkin River at this point, so be prepared to share the road with the trucks, which must also cross. Fortunately, there's a narrow shoulder and the pavement is smooth. On the left, you'll pass Cooleemee Plantation, an excellent example of Anglo-Grecian architecture. The next community is Fork Church.

After you passs Twin Lakes Airport on the slightly rolling Fork Bixby Road, you cross railroad tracks at Cornatzer Road. Watch out for bad railroad tracks both here and on Milling Road. After you cross N.C. 801 on Farmington Road, be sure to notice the historic houses lining that portion of the route. Courtney-Huntsville/Shallowford Road brings you back across the Yadkin to The Oaks Shopping Center.

Mile-by-Mile Directions	Distance to Next Turn	Total Distance
From The Oaks Shopping Center, turn LEFT onto Shallowford Road (SR 1001). Continue on Shallowford Road to Lewisville-Clemmons Road (SR 1156).	0.5	0.5
Turn RIGHT on Lewisville-Clemmons Road and ride to Lawrence Ridge Road in Clemmons.	0.7	1.2
Turn RIGHT on Lawrence Ridge Road and go to Divaldi Street.	0.1	1.3
Turn LEFT on Divaldi Street and continue to the stop sign at Reynolds Road (SR 1160).	0.3	1.6
Turn RIGHT on Reynolds Road, where there is a sharp left curve. Continue to the stop sign at Styers Ferry Road (SR 1100).	0.9	2.5
Turn RIGHT on Styers Ferry Road and ride to Harper Road (SR 1101).	0.3	2.8
Turn LEFT on Harper Road and go to the stop sign at Peace Haven Road (SR 1891).	2.2	5.0
Turn LEFT on Peace Haven Road and continue to the stoplight at Lewisville-Clemmons Road (SR 1103).	0.4	5.4
Turn RIGHT on Lewisville-Clemmons Road and go through the town of Clemmons to Stadium Drive. You'll come to Stadium Drive just after passing the Etna station on the left.	0.8	6.2

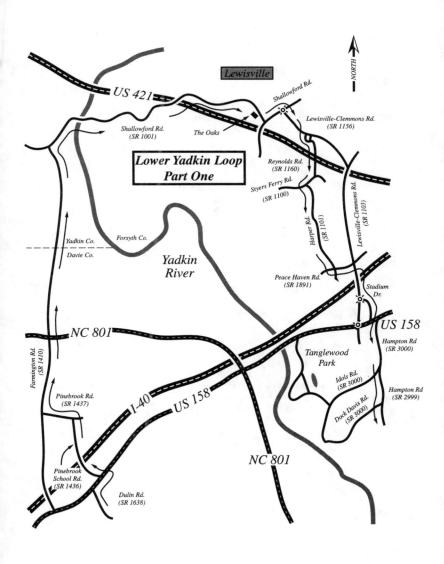

Mile-by-Mile Directions	Distance to Next Turn	Total Distance
Turn LEFT on Stadium Drive at the traffic signal and go to the stop sign at Clemmons Road.	0.8	7.0
Turn LEFT on Clemmons Road and go to the traffic signal at Hampton Road (SR 3000).	0.1	7.1
Turn RIGHT on Hampton Road and ride to Old Mill Farm Road (SR 1445).	7.8	14.9
Turn RIGHT on Old Mill Farm Road and go to the stop sign at Friendship Church Road (SR 1441).	3.4	18.3
Turn RIGHT on Friendship Church Road and travel to the stop sign at Yadkin College Road (SR 1194).	2.2	20.5
Turn RIGHT on Yadkin College Road and continue to Koontz Road (SR 1186).	0.4	20.9
Turn LEFT on Koontz Road and go to the stop sign at U.S. 64.	1.3	22.2
Turn RIGHT on U.S. 64 and go to N.C. 801.	3.9	26.1
CROSS N.C. 801 and continue to Fork Bixby Road (SR 1611), which is the first street on the right after the airport sign.	0.1	26.2
Turn RIGHT on Fork Bixby Road and ride to the stop sign at Cornatzer Road (SR 1616).	4.3	30.5
Turn LEFT on Cornatzer Road and go to Milling Road (SR 1600).	2.0	32.5
Turn RIGHT on Milling Road and travel to Dulin Road (SR 1638).	1.1	33.6

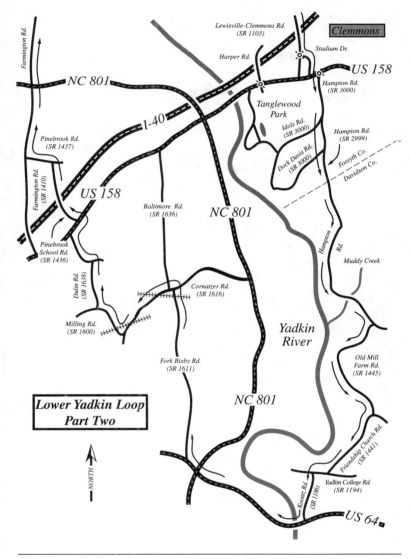

Farmington Rd.

Lewisville-Clemmons Rd.
(SR 1103)

Clemmons

Stadium Dr.

Harper Rd.

NC 801

US 158

Hampton Rd.
(SR 3000)

Tanglewood
Park

I-40

Pinebrook Rd.
(SR 1437)

Idols Rd.
(SR 3000)

Hampton Rd.
(SR 2999)

Dock Davis Rd.
(SR 3000)

Forsyth Co.

Davidson Co.

Farmington Rd.
(SR 1410)

US 158

Baltimore Rd.
(SR 1636)

NC 801

Hampton Rd.

Pinebrook
School Rd.
(SR 1436)

Muddy Creek

Dulin Rd.
(SR 1638)

Cornatzer Rd.
(SR 1616)

Yadkin
River

Milling Rd.
(SR 1600)

Old Mill
Farm Rd.
(SR 1445)

Fork Bixby Rd.
(SR 1611)

**Lower Yadkin Loop
Part Two**

NC 801

Friendship Church Rd.
(SR 1441)

← NORTH

Koontz Rd.
(SR 1186)

Yadkin College Rd.
(SR 1194)

US 64

Mile-by-Mile Directions	Distance to Next Turn	Total Distance
Turn RIGHT on Dulin Road and go to the fork in the road.	1.2	34.8
BEAR left at the fork to stay on Dulin Road. Continue to the stop sign at U.S. 158.	1.1	35.9
Turn RIGHT on U.S. 158 and ride to Pinebrook School Road (SR 1436).	0.7	36.6
Turn LEFT on Pinebrook School Road and travel to the stop sign at Pinebrook Road (SR 1437). Gilbert Road goes off to the right.	2.0	38.6
Turn LEFT on Pinebrook Road and continue to the stop sign at Farmington Road (SR 1410).	0.8	39.4
Turn RIGHT on Farmington Road and go to the stop sign at N.C. 801.	2.1	41.5
CROSS N.C. 801 and stay on Farmington Road (the road number changes to SR 1716) to the stop sign at Courtney-Huntsville Road (SR 1001).	4.6	46.1
Turn RIGHT on Courtney-Huntsville/ Shallowford Road and ride to The Oaks Shopping Center on the right.	6.6	52.7

Short Lower Yadkin Ride

Description of the route

This ride starts in Tanglewood Park. The easiest place to park is at Mallard Lake. From that parking area, you take a left turn onto the main road that leads to the back gate. You exit the park on Idols Road, which makes a ninety-degree turn across some railroad tracks. At that point, the road changes its name to Dock Davis Road. The scenery along this portion changes from pastures to woods. Hampton Road has a smooth surface and is fairly level. One neighbor along this road collects farm implements and equipment. You can see the rusty hulks sulking next to the road. After riding 4.6 miles, you come upon large, elegant homes. Atop a hill on the right, the home with a dark fence around it belongs to race-car owner Richard Childress.

Old Mill Farm Road passes mainly through residential areas but also straddles pastures for horses. Friendship Church Road leads to Yadkin College Road. Koontz Road is rolling, with a variety of ups and downs. The Texaco station on the left at U.S. 64 makes a good rest stop. It even has a bench for weary cyclists. U.S. 64 is a very busy road with lots of

Starting point
   The back entrance to Tangle-wood Park
Distance
   32.7 miles
Terrain
   Rolling to hilly
Food and drinks
   Tanglewood Park; Texaco station and Tarheel Hot Dogs on U.S. 64
Recommendations
   Certain sections have heavy traffic.

trucks, but it does have a narrow shoulder. No double pacelines here! Fork Bixby Road is the first road on the right after you cross N.C. 801. There's a sign for Twin Oaks Airport right beside the road. Fork Bixby has cattle pastures and some large vegetable gardens. Baltimore Road is a level road with wide, sweeping vistas. This section is called the airstrip because a fast paceline can really fly. A large Reynolds Tobacco facility, used for tobacco storage, is on the left. You travel slightly downhill on U.S. 158 until you make a small climb to reach N.C. 801. Next, you pass the town of Bermuda Run before you cross the river and reach the main entrance to Tanglewood Park. The entrance fee for Tanglewood is $2.00 per vehicle.

Mile-by-Mile Directions	Distance to Next Turn	Total Distance
From the back gate at Tanglewood Park, turn RIGHT on Idols Road (SR 3000) and go to the ninety-degree turn at the railroad tracks.	0.9	0.9
Bear LEFT on Dock Davis Road (SR 3000) and go to the stop sign at Hampton Road (SR 2999).	2.9	3.8
Turn RIGHT on Hampton Road and ride to Old Mill Farm Road (SR 1445).	5.4	9.2
Turn RIGHT on Old Mill Farm Road and go to Friendship Church Road (SR 1441).	3.4	12.6
Turn RIGHT on Friendship Church Road and travel to the stop sign at Yadkin College Road (SR 1194).	2.2	14.8
Turn RIGHT on Yadkin College Road and continue to Koontz Road (SR 1186).	0.4	15.2
Turn LEFT on Koontz Road and go to the stop sign at U.S. 64.	1.3	16.5
Turn RIGHT on U.S. 64 and ride to Fork Bixby Road (SR 1611).	4.0	20.5

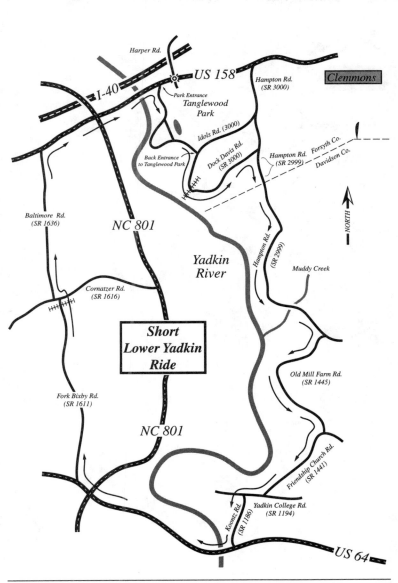

Mile-by-Mile Directions	Distance to Next Turn	Total Distance
Turn RIGHT on Fork Bixby Road and travel to Cornatzer Road (SR 1606).	4.3	24.8
Turn LEFT on Cornatzer Road and continue to Baltimore Road (SR 1636).	0.1	24.9
Turn RIGHT on Baltimore Road and go to the stop sign at U.S. 158.	3.0	27.9
Turn RIGHT on U.S. 158 and ride to the signal at N.C. 801. Note: U.S. 158 from N.C. 801 to the entrance to Tanglewood Park has dense traffic. The Kathryn Crosby Bridge, which crosses the Yadkin River, is narrow and can have a rough road surface. Be careful! There is no shoulder on the bridge and no place to go if you have problems.	1.5	29.4
CROSS N.C. 801 to Tanglewood Park, which is on the right. Follow Tanglewood Drive until you pass the swimming pool on the right. Turn left and ride toward the golf course. Mallard Lake is on the left.	3.3	32.7

Biathlon Time Trial Route

Starting point
Mallard Lake at Tanglewood Park

Distance
26.4 miles

Terrain
Rolling, with some hills

Food and drinks
Tanglewood Park

Recommendations
Have two dollars with you for the entrance fee to Tanglewood; otherwise, you can park just outside the back gate to the park.

Description of the route

When some of the local charitable organizations stage a biathlon, this is the current route they like to use for the cycling portion. You'll see a painted X in the road where the 40-kilometer time trial usually turns around. The roads behind Tanglewood have little traffic, although that may change as the area around Salem Glen Country Club develops. After your turn onto Hampton Road, the scenery becomes somewhat more rural, with landscapes alternating between pastures and wooded areas. Hampton Road has a smooth surface and is fairly level.

Along this part of the route, you'll see someone's collection of large, rusting farm implements and equipment—a tribute to the historic use of the land in these parts. About 4.6 miles along Hampton Road, you'll come upon several huge estates on both sides of the road. Richard Childress, the famous race-car owner, built the large house on the hill with the dark fence around the property to the right.

Old Mill Farm Road has scattered residences, mixed with fields for grazing horses. The intersection with Friendship Church Road is the turn-around point for the biathlon. If you're interested in riding farther, check out the Short Lower Yadkin Ride.

Mile-by-Mile Directions	Distance to Next Turn	Total Distance
From Mallard Lake, ride on Lake Mallard Lane to the stop sign. Turn LEFT and go past the golf course to Tanglewood's back gate.	0.6	0.6
Turn RIGHT on Idols Road (SR 3000) and go to the 90-degree turn at the railroad tracks.	0.9	1.5
The road bears LEFT onto Dock Davis Road (still SR 3000). Continue on Dock Davis Road to the stop sign at Hampton Road (SR 2999).	2.9	4.4
Turn RIGHT on Hampton Road and ride to Old Mill Farm Road (SR 1445).	5.4	9.8
Turn RIGHT on Old Mill Farm Road and travel to Friendship Church Road (SR 1441).	3.4	13.2

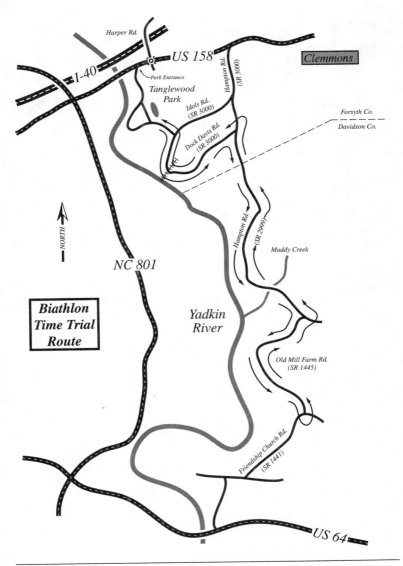

Mile-by-Mile Directions	Distance to Next Turn	Total Distance
TURN AROUND at Friendship Church Road and return on Old Mill Farm Road to Hampton Road.	3.4	16.6
Turn LEFT on Hampton Road and ride to Dock Davis Road.	5.4	22.0
Turn LEFT on Dock Davis Road and go to Idols Road.	2.9	24.9
Bear RIGHT on Idols Road and ride to the back entrance to Tanglewood Park.	0.9	25.8
Turn LEFT into the park. Turn RIGHT on Lake Mallard Lane and go to Mallard Lake.	0.6	26.4

Waterworks Loop

Description of the route

This route gives a glimpse of how well some of Winston-Salem's foremost citizens lived. The ride starts in Reynolda Village, formerly part of the huge estate of Richard Joshua Reynolds, founder of Reynolds Tobacco Company. It then crosses Reynolda Road into Graylyn Conference Center, formerly the estate of Bowman Gray, Sr. At one time, Gray was the chief executive at Reynolds Tobacco. Gray bought the land for Graylyn from Mr. Reynolds. Designed to look like a French chateau, the house now serves as the main part of the conference center that is owned by Wake Forest University.

The route then passes through the Buena Vista neighborhood before crossing Stratford Road into the Ardmore neighborhood. Once you cross Silas Creek Parkway on Ebert Street, you'll be amazed at how quickly you leave the city and find yourself in the midst of beautiful rolling farmland. The vista from the top of the hill on Fraternity Church Road is magnificent, with carefully maintained farms and homes on large acreage spread all around you. Along Cooper Road, the views are broken by woods. The big hill you

Starting point
   Ken's Bike Shop in Reynolda Village
Distance
   32.3 miles
Terrain
   Rolling
Food and drinks
   Reynolda Village; along Country Club Road
Recommendations
   This route is not good during morning or evening rush hours.

approach next forewarns of a stream nearby. Just before you come to the stop at Frye Bridge Road, the county bike route goes off to the right.

This ride is named for the water treatment plant you'll see at the intersection of Frye Bridge and Cooper Roads. Hampton Road, which leads into Clemmons, is fairly busy. U.S. 158 is a five-lane road with lots of traffic at certain times. Fortunately, you're on U.S. 158 only a short distance. Kinnamon Road has a wide, smooth surface and a great view of Sauratown Mountain. There is some traffic on Kinnamon Road, but the speed limit is only 45 miles per hour. Before you head up the nice hill on Kinnamon Road, you will see a small scenic lake off to the right.

You continue on Peace Haven Road past the West Forsyth YMCA's facility to Harper Road. Once you turn right on Lewisville-Clemmons Road, you're on the stretch known as the "airstrip" because it's a fast, downhill section. It pays to make good time on this busy stretch of road. Next comes Alamo Street. Perhaps this street got its name because Davy Crockett must have died on this hill. It doesn't look like much of an uphill but halfway up, you'll feel like you're climbing a pole. At least this keeps you off busy Country Club Road for a bit.

Country Club Road is a wide, three-lane street, which is generally fairly nice for cyclists. However, the section between Peace Haven and Jonestown Roads is the most dangerous because of the large number of driveways. Don't try to set a time-trial record on this part or you'll be quickly separated from your bike. Through this section, keep your hands on your brakes and expect people to pull out. Fortunately, you're only on this road for a short distance, then the traffic thins out a bit as you move toward town.

When you get back to Reynolda House, you can walk your bike through a pedestrian entrance if the gates are closed. Just after you pass the main house on your right, you have the option of returning to Ken's Bike Shop by going through the stanchions in the road on the right or by continuing on the main road as described in the mile-by-mile instructions.

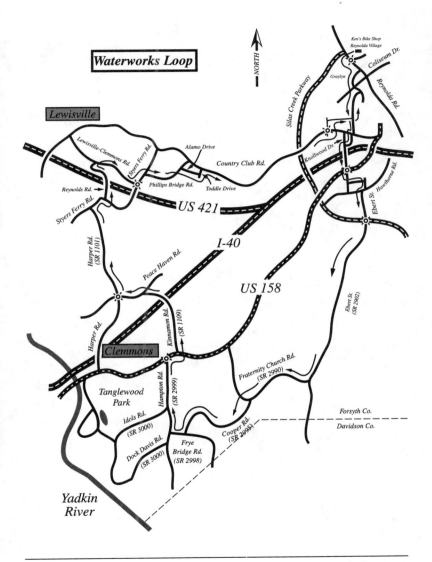

Waterworks Loop

NORTH

Ken's Bike Shop
Reynolda Village

Coliseum Dr.

Graylyn

Reynolda Rd.

Silas Creek Parkway

Lewisville

Lewisville-Clemmons Rd.

Styers Ferry Rd.

Alamo Drive

Country Club Rd.

Knollwood Dr.

Reynolds Rd.

Phillips Bridge Rd.

Toddle Drive

Styers Ferry Rd.

Ebert St.

Hawthorne Rd.

US 421

I-40

US 158

Harper Rd. (SR 1101)

Peace Haven Rd.

Ebert St. (SR 2902)

Harper Rd.

Kinnamon Rd. (SR 1109)

Clemmons

Tanglewood Park

Hampton Rd. (SR 2999)

Fraternity Church Rd. (SR 2990)

Idols Rd. (SR 3000)

Dock Davis Rd. (SR 3000)

Frye Bridge Rd. (SR 2998)

Cooper Rd. (SR 2953)

Forsyth Co.

Davidson Co.

Yadkin River

Mile-by-Mile Directions	Distance to Next Turn	Total Distance
From Ken's Bike Shop, go through Reynolda Village to the signal at the main entrance to the village at Reynolda Road. Turn LEFT on Reynolda Road and go to the entrance of Graylyn Conference Center.	0.6	0.6
Turn RIGHT into the grounds of the Graylyn Conference Center. BEAR LEFT to go past the main house, then continue to the LEFT to the stop sign at Coliseum Drive.	0.4	1.0
CROSS Coliseum Drive onto Oaklawn Avenue and go to Arbor Road.	0.1	1.1
Turn RIGHT on Arbor Road. Continue on Arbor Road, crossing Robinhood, Buena Vista, and Warwick Roads until you reach the stop sign at Country Club Road.	1.2	2.3
Turn RIGHT on Country Club Road, and take an immediate LEFT onto Greenwich Road. Continue on Greenwich Road to Knollwood Street.	0.5	2.8
Turn LEFT on Knollwood Street and cross Business 40 and Stratford Road. There is a bad railroad crossing on Knollwood Street. Continue on Knollwood Street to Queen Street.	0.5	3.3
Turn LEFT on Queen Street and go to a four-way stop at Melrose Avenue.	0.6	3.9
Turn RIGHT on Melrose Street and ride to Hawthorne Road.	0.5	4.4
Turn RIGHT on Hawthorne Road and travel to Ebert Street.	0.2	4.6
Turn LEFT on Ebert Street and continue across Silas Creek Parkway to Clemmonsville Road.	3.8	8.4

Mile-by-Mile Directions	Distance to Next Turn	Total Distance
CROSS Clemmonsville Road on Ebert Street and travel to Fraternity Church Road (SR 2990).	1.0	9.4
Turn RIGHT on Fraternity Church Road and go to Cooper Road (SR 2995).	2.0	11.4
Turn LEFT on Cooper Road and continue to the stop sign at Frye Bridge Road (SR 2998).	1.5	12.9
Turn RIGHT on Frye Bridge Road and ride to the stop sign at Hampton Road (SR 2999).	1.2	14.1
Turn RIGHT on Hampton Road and travel into Clemmons. Continue to the signal at U.S. 158.	1.9	16.0
Turn RIGHT on U.S. 158 and ride to Kinnamon Road (SR 1109).	0.3	16.3
Turn LEFT on Kinnamon Road and go to Peace Haven Road (SR 1891).	1.8	18.1
Turn LEFT on Peace Haven Road. At the stoplight, CROSS Lewisville-Clemmons Road (SR 1103) and go to Harper Road (SR 1101).	0.5	18.6
Turn RIGHT on Harper Road and ride to Styers Ferry Road (SR 1100).	2.3	20.9
Turn RIGHT on Styers Ferry Road and travel to Reynolds Road (SR 1160).	0.3	21.2
Turn LEFT on Reynolds Road and go to Lewisville-Clemmons Road.	1.0	22.2
Turn RIGHT on Lewisville-Clemmons Road and continue to the stop sign at the westbound ramp for U.S. 421.	1.3	23.5

Mile-by-Mile Directions	Distance to Next Turn	Total Distance
Turn LEFT on the westbound ramp and go to the signal. Turn LEFT on Styers Ferry Road (which is now SR 1103) and ride to Phillips Bridge Road (SR 1152).	0.5	24.0
Turn RIGHT on Phillips Bridge Road and ride to Alamo Drive.	1.1	25.1
Turn RIGHT on Alamo Drive and travel to Toddle Drive.	0.4	25.5
Turn LEFT on Toddle Drive and go to Country Club Road. Turn RIGHT on Country Club Road and go to Westview Drive.	4.2	29.7
Turn LEFT on Westview Drive and go to the signal at Forest Drive.	0.2	29.9
Turn RIGHT on Forest Drive and ride to Arbor Road.	0.6	30.5
Turn LEFT on Arbor Road and CROSS Robinhood Road. Continue on Arbor Road to Oaklawn Drive.	0.8	31.3
Turn LEFT on Oaklawn Avenue and CROSS Coliseum Drive into the grounds at Graylyn. BEAR RIGHT to Reynolda Road.	0.4	31.7
CROSS Reynolda Road into the Reynolda House grounds.	0.4	32.1
CONTINUE on the road as it bears LEFT into Reynolda Village. Once in the village, BEAR RIGHT to Ken's Bike Shop.	0.2	32.3

Tour of Tanglewood

Description of the route

The beginning and end of this route covers the same roads as the Waterworks Loop. Dock Davis Road is busy because of Salem Glen Golf Course, which you'll see off to your left. Just before the curve, the railroad tracks are at a slight angle, so take care when you cross them to reach the back entrance of Tanglewood Park. The gates at Tanglewood are frequently closed, but you can walk your bike through the pedestrian opening at the side of the gates.

Starting point
   Ken's Bike Shop in Reynolda Village
Distance
   33.0 miles (plus whatever miles you choose to ride within Tanglewood)
Terrain
   Rolling, with a few hills
Food and drinks
   Reynolda Village; along Country Club Road; Tanglewood Park
Recommendations
   This is not a good ride during morning or evening rush hours.

The highlight of this ride is the tour of Tanglewood Park, a 1,300-acre recreational facility. Formerly the country estate of William Reynolds and his wife, the park was bequeathed to the county. Its facilities include tennis courts, a 36-hole golf course, a par-3 course, stables, picnic areas, and paddleboat and canoe rentals. The park has recently added mountain bike trails. (See "Mountain Bike Trails" section.)

One point of interest in the park is the rose garden next to the Manor House. There are also huge specimens of ancient oaks in the gardens around the Manor House. The small country church near the golf clubhouse takes you back to a simpler time. This spot is popular for small weddings. Whatever time you choose to spend here will offer a cool respite from travails.

The route back into Winston-Salem snakes primarily through residential areas between Lewisville and Clemmons in the western part of Forsyth County.

Mile-by-Mile Directions	Distance to Next Turn	Total Distance
From Ken's Bike Shop, go through Reynolda Village to the signal at the main entrance to the village at Reynolda Road. Turn LEFT on Reynolda Road to enter Graylyn Conference Center.	0.6	0.6
Turn RIGHT into the grounds of the Graylyn Conference Center. BEAR LEFT to go past the main house. Continue to the stop sign at Coliseum Drive.	0.4	1.0
CROSS Coliseum Drive onto Oaklawn Avenue and go to Arbor Road.	0.1	1.1
Turn RIGHT on Arbor Road. Continue on Arbor Road, crossing Robinhood, Buena Vista, and Warwick Roads until you reach the stop sign at Country Club Road.	1.2	2.3
Turn RIGHT on Country Club Road, then take an immediate LEFT on Greenwich Road and continue to Knollwood Street.	0.5	2.8
Turn LEFT on Knollwood Street, CROSS Business 40 and Stratford Road, where there is a bad railroad crossing. Continue on Knollwood Street to Queen Street.	0.5	3.3
Turn LEFT on Queen Street and go to the four-way stop at Melrose Street.	0.6	3.9

Mile-by-Mile Directions	Distance to Next Turn	Total Distance
Turn RIGHT on Melrose Street and ride to Hawthorne Road.	0.5	4.4
Turn RIGHT on Hawthorne Road and go to Ebert Street.	0.2	4.6
Turn LEFT on Ebert Street and continue across Silas Creek Parkway to Clemmonsville Road.	3.8	8.4
CROSS Clemmonsville Road on Ebert Street to Fraternity Church Road (SR 2990).	1.0	9.4
Turn RIGHT on Fraternity Church Road and go to Cooper Road (SR 2995).	2.0	11.4
Turn LEFT on Cooper Road and ride to the stop sign at Frye Bridge Road (SR 2998).	1.5	12.9
Turn RIGHT on Frye Bridge Road and travel to the stop sign at Hampton Road (SR 2999).	1.2	14.1
Turn LEFT on Hampton Road and go to Dock Davis Road (SR 3000).	0.2	14.3
Turn RIGHT on Dock Davis Road and ride to the railroad tracks.	2.0	16.3
CROSS the railroad tracks and follow the right curve. The name of the road changes to Idols Road (which is now SR 3000), although there is no street sign. Continue on Idols Road to the back entrance to Tanglewood Park.	0.9	17.2

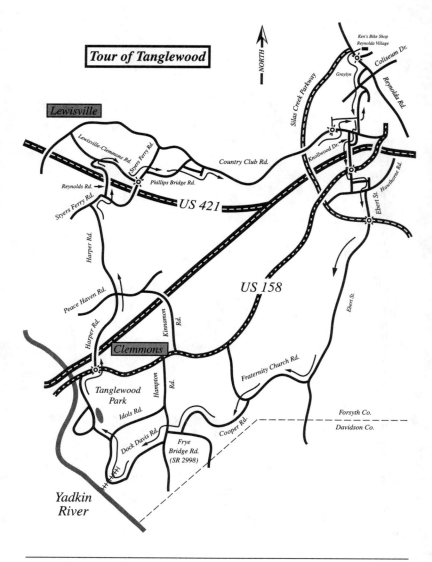

Tour of Tanglewood

Lewisville

Lewisville-Clemmons Rd.

Styers Ferry Rd.

Country Club Rd.

Reynolds Rd.

Phillips Bridge Rd.

Styers Ferry Rd.

US 421

Harper Rd.

Peace Haven Rd.

Harper Rd.

Kinnamon Rd.

US 158

Clemmons

Tanglewood Park

Hampton Rd.

Idols Rd.

Fraternity Church Rd.

Dock Davis Rd.

Frye Bridge Rd. (SR 2998)

Cooper Rd.

Forsyth Co.

Davidson Co.

Yadkin River

NORTH

Ken's Bike Shop
Reynolda Village

Coliseum Dr.

Graylyn

Silas Creek Parkway

Reynolda Rd.

Knollwood Dr.

Ebert St.

Hawthorne Rd.

Ebert St.

Mile-by-Mile Directions	Distance to Next Turn	Total Distance
Turn LEFT into the back entrance of Tanglewood Park. You will pass the golf course and Mallard Lake. When you reach the intersection with Tanglewood Drive, turn RIGHT and ride past the swimming pool, tennis courts, manor house, stables, and welcome center to the front entrance of the park. Continue to U.S. 158, where you will turn RIGHT on U.S. 158 and ride to Harper Road (SR 1101). Turn LEFT on Harper Road and go to Styers Ferry Road (SR 1100).	0.4	17.6
Turn LEFT on Harper Road and go to Styers Ferry Road (SR 1100).	4.0	21.6
Turn RIGHT on Styers Ferry and travel to Reynolds Road (SR 1160).	0.3	21.9
Turn LEFT on Reynolds Road and ride to Lewisville-Clemmons Road (SR 1156).	1.0	22.9
Turn RIGHT on Lewisville-Clemmons Road and go to the stop sign at the westbound ramp to U.S. 421.	1.3	24.2
Turn LEFT on the westbound ramp and ride to the signal at Styers Ferry Road, which is now SR 1103. Turn LEFT on Styers Ferry Road and ride to Phillips Bridge Road (SR 1152).	0.5	24.7
Turn RIGHT on Phillips Bridge Road and go to Alamo Drive.	1.1	25.8
Turn RIGHT on Alamo Drive and travel to Toddle Drive.	0.4	26.2
Turn LEFT on Toddle Drive and go to Country Club Road. Turn RIGHT on Country Club Road and ride to Westview Drive.	4.2	30.4

Mile-by-Mile Directions	Distance to Next Turn	Total Distance
At the signal, turn LEFT on Westview Drive and ride to Forest Drive.	0.2	30.6
Turn RIGHT on Forest Drive and ride to Arbor Road.	0.6	31.2
Turn LEFT on Arbor Road and CROSS Robinhood Road to Oaklawn Drive.	0.8	32.0
Turn LEFT on Oaklawn Avenue and CROSS Coliseum Drive into the grounds at Graylyn. BEAR RIGHT and go to Reynolda Road.	0.4	32.4
CROSS Reynolda Road into the Reynolda House grounds.	0.4	32.8
CONTINUE on this road, bearing LEFT into Reynolda Village. Turn RIGHT once in the village to reach Ken's Bike Shop.	0.2	33.0

Meadowlark Loop

Description of the route

This pleasant, in-town loop is a good ride when time is short. It covers some of the Winston-Salem's key attractions—Wake Forest University, Reynolda House Museum of American Art, and Graylyn Conference Center. When you leave Ken's Bike Shop, you have two options. If traffic is heavy on Reynolda Road, you can ride through the grounds of Reynolda House to the main entrance, which is across from Graylyn. You'll be traveling against car traffic, so take care. If traffic is not heavy on Reynolda Road, you can use this route to reach Graylyn.

Both Reynolda House and the grounds of Graylyn Conference Center are like oases in the middle of this busy city. From Graylyn, this route takes you past the lovely older homes of Buena Vista (pronounced Byou-na Vistah by the locals) to Country Club Road. This road is as close to a boulevard as they come—a nice, wide tree-shaded road much of the way. You'll take Country Club Road to a point close to where it changes to Shallowford Road. A right turn on Meadowlark Drive takes you past two new schools and new housing developments, which were built on property

Starting point
   Ken's Bike Shop in Reynolda Village
Distance
   17.4 miles
Terrain
   Rolling, with a few good climbs
Food and drinks
   Reynolda Village, along Country Club Road
Recommendations
   It is best not to take this ride at rush hours.

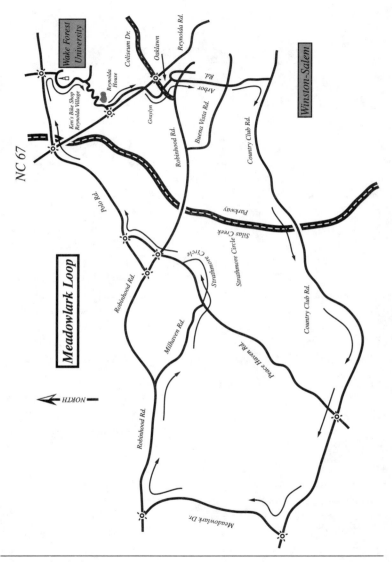

formerly owned by the Bowman Gray family. Bowman Gray, Sr. and Jr. both served as head of Reynolds Tobacco Company at one time. The new developments have brought more traffic along this road.

To avoid busy Robinhood Road as much as possible, take Milhaven Road. It has a nasty uphill, but it is more pleasant nonetheless. Peace Haven and Polo Roads will lead you to Wake Forest University and back to Ken's Bike Shop. By the way, Polo Road got its name because the old polo fields were located where Speas School is now.

Mile-by-Mile Directions	Distance to Next Turn	Total Distance
From Ken's Bike Shop, follow the main street toward the main entrance to Reynolda Village. Bear LEFT instead of turning right where the median just inside the village is located. Ride past Reynolda House to the main entrance gates at Reynolda Road. Traffic will be driving in the opposite direction on the Reynolda House grounds, so stay alert.	0.5	0.5
CROSS Reynolda Road and ride into Graylyn Conference Center. Pass in front of the main house, then turn LEFT at the fork and go to the stop sign Coliseum Drive.	0.4	0.9
CROSS Coliseum Drive onto Oaklawn Avenue. Continue on Oaklawn Avenue to the stop sign at Arbor Road.	0.1	1.0
Turn RIGHT on Arbor Road. Continuing on Arbor Road, CROSS Robinhood, Buena Vista and Warwick Roads. Ride until you reach the stop sign at Country Club Road.	1.2	2.2
Turn RIGHT on Country Club Road (SR 1001) and go to Meadowlark Drive (SR 1314).	5.9	8.1

Mile-by-Mile Directions	Distance to Next Turn	Total Distance
Turn RIGHT on Meadowlark Drive and continue to Robinhood Road (SR 1348).	2.0	10.1
Turn RIGHT on Robinhood Road and travel to Milhaven Road.	1.4	11.5
Turn RIGHT on Milhaven Road and go to Peace Haven Road.	1.3	12.8
Turn LEFT on Peace Haven Road, and take an immediate RIGHT onto Strathmore Circle. Continue on Strathmore Circle to Peace Haven Road.	0.3	13.1
Turn RIGHT on Peace Haven Road and go to Robinhood Road.	0.5	13.6
Using the traffic signal, CROSS Robinhood Road and ride to Polo Road.	0.6	14.2
Turn RIGHT on Polo Road and go to Wingate Road.	2.3	16.5
Turn RIGHT on Wingate Road and travel to Wake Forest Road.	0.2	16.7
Turn RIGHT on Wake Forest Road, which circles past Wait Chapel before turning to the right. Continue on Wake Forest Road to the three-way stop.	0.4	17.1
Turn RIGHT on Wake Forest Road, then take an immediate LEFT onto Faculty Drive. On the RIGHT you will see the path that leads through stone columns to Reynolda Village and Ken's Bike Shop.	0.3	17.4

Inside Loop

Starting point
Ken's Bike Shop in Reynolda Village

Distance
13.5 miles

Terrain
Undulates slightly, with a few hills

Food and drinks
Reynolda Village; along Country Club Road; at the intersection of Peace Haven and Country Club Roads

Recommendations
Avoid Country Club Road during rush hours.

Description of the route

This is a good in-town training ride, when time is short. The sections on busier streets are interspersed with residential sections that have less traffic. Riding through the grounds of Reynolda House and Graylyn offers a nice respite and a taste of how two of Winston-Salem's wealthiest families once lived.

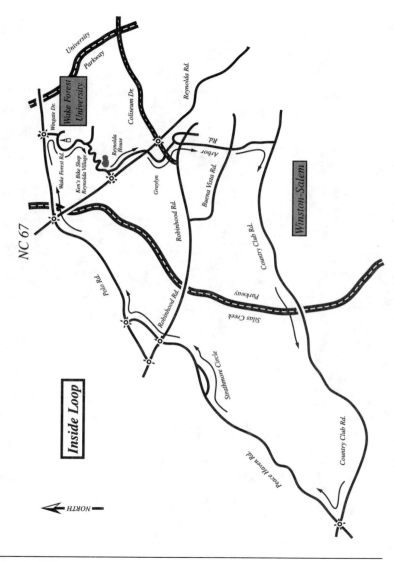

The route traverses the streets of Buena Vista, one of Winston-Salem's earliest suburbs. The older homes that line these streets have undergone a refurbishment as younger families move in. Country Club Road is wide, but traffic gets busier as you approach the hill to Peace Haven Road. Although you might be tempted to tuck and race on the downhill stretch, watch for cars pulling out along this section. Keep your hands on your brake hoods here!

Peace Haven Road is busy but wide enough that cars can pass easily. Strathmore Circle allows you to avoid a big hill and a bad curve, where joggers have been killed. Polo Road then leads you back to Wake Forest University and the path back to Ken's Bike Shop.

Mile-by-Mile Directions	Distance to Next Turn	Total Distance
From Ken's Bike Shop follow the main street toward the main entrance to Reynolda Village. Bear LEFT instead of turning right where the median just inside the village is located. Ride past Reynolda House to the main entrance gates at Reynolda Road. Caution: The traffic will be driving in the opposite direction on Reynolda House grounds, so stay alert.	0.6	0.6
CROSS Reynolda Road into the Graylyn Conference Center. Pass in front of the main house, then turn LEFT at the fork and go to the stop sign at Coliseum Drive.	0.4	1.0
CROSS Coliseum Drive onto Oaklawn Avenue. Continue on Oaklawn Avenue to the stop sign at Arbor Road.	0.1	1.1
Turn RIGHT on Arbor Road. Continuing on Arbor Road, CROSS Robinhood, Buena Vista, and Warwick Roads. Ride until you reach the stop sign at Country Club Road.	1.2	2.3

Mile-by-Mile Directions	Distance to Next Turn	Total Distance
Turn RIGHT on Country Club Road and ride to Peace Haven Road.	4.5	6.8
Turn RIGHT on Peace Haven Road and travel to Strathmore Circle.	2.1	8.9
Turn RIGHT on Strathmore Circle and go to the stop sign at Peace Haven Road.	0.3	9.2
Turn RIGHT on Peace Haven and go to Polo Road.	1.2	10.4
Turn RIGHT on Polo Road and ride to Reynolda Road.	1.4	11.8
CROSS Reynolda Road on Polo Road and travel to Wingate Road.	0.8	12.6
Turn RIGHT on Wingate Road and continue to Wake Forest Road.	0.2	12.8
Turn RIGHT on Wake Forest Road, which circles past Wait Chapel before turning to the right. Continue on Wake Forest Road to a three-way stop sign.	0.4	13.2
Turn RIGHT on Wake Forest Road, then take an immediate LEFT onto Faculty Drive. You will see the path that leads through stone columns to Reynolda Village and Ken's Bike Shop on the right.	0.3	13.5

Tour of Baux Mountain

Description of the route

While the first part of this route has some traffic, the countryside views that follow are well worth the trouble. The path from Reynolda Village to Wake Forest University passes through a lovely forest glen. The path is popular with joggers and people out for a leisurely stroll, so take care to announce your approach. You don't want to startle someone into your path. The ride through Wake Forest's campus is pleasant, but watch out for those huge speed bumps. At least you don't have to worry about speeding cars.

Although they are busy, Polo Road and Indiana Avenue have five lanes, so choose a lane and behave like a vehicle. Motor Road is narrow and hilly, but there's usually not a lot of traffic. Baux Mountain Road crosses Old Hollow Road (N.C. 66) at an angle that makes visibility poor, so take care! If you want a place to catch your breath and get a drink, there's a convenience store on the left. The next section of Baux Mountain Road is curvy, with some slight ups and

Starting point
 Ken's Bike Shop in Reynolda Village
Distance
 26.2 miles
Terrain
 Rolling
Food and drinks
 Reynolda Village; convenience store at the intersection of Baux Mountain and Old Hollow Roads
Recommendations
 This ride is not a good ride during morning or evening rush hours.

, but the many trees lining the road will make you feel as though you've left the city far behind.

This stretch of Baux Mountain Road takes you past the road that leads to Lake Woussicket. It gives you great views of Sauratown Mountain on the left. From the top of Baux Mountain, the road's namesake, there's a great 180-degree view of the Sauratown range. To the right, you'll pass Memorial Industrial Road, which leads to Horizons Park and Germanton Road (N.C. 8). The section of Red Bank Road that follows is lined with a profusion of black-eyed Susans and Queen Anne's lace during the summer. It's definitely a pleasant break from the city.

Mile-by-Mile Directions	Distance to Next Turn	Total Distance
From Ken's Bike Shop, take the hill down toward the lake and bear LEFT.	0.1	0.1
Take a right onto the path from Reynolda Village that crosses Lake Katherine to Wake Forest University.	0.2	0.3
Turn LEFT on Faculty Drive and go to the stop sign at Wake Forest Road. Turn RIGHT on Wake Forest Road and continue to the three-way stop across from Salem Hall.	50 feet	0.3
Turn LEFT on Wake Forest Road and wind around the campus, past Wait Chapel to Wingate Drive.	0.4	0.7
Turn LEFT on Wingate Drive and ride to the signal at Polo Road.	0.2	0.9
Turn RIGHT on Polo Road and CROSS Cherry Street to the signal at Indiana Avenue.	1.4	2.3
Turn LEFT on Indiana Avenue and go to Motor Road.	0.1	2.4
Turn RIGHT on Motor Road. At the signal, CROSS Patterson Avenue and continue on Motor Road.	0.9	3.3

Mile-by-Mile Directions	Distance to Next Turn	Total Distance
CROSS Ogburn Avenue and Old Rural Hall Road as you continue on Motor Road to the stop sign at Baux Mountain Road (SR 2211).	1.4	4.7
Turn LEFT on Baux Mountain Road (road number changes to SR 1946) and ride to the stop sign at Old Hollow Road (N.C. 66).	2.3	7.0
CONTINUE straight on Baux Mountain Road to the intersection with Red Bank Road (SR 1917).	1.1	8.1
Bear RIGHT on Baux Mountain Road and ride to Kiger Road (SR 1942).	3.9	12.0
Turn LEFT on Kiger Road and go to N.C. 65.	1.6	13.6
Turn LEFT on N.C. 65 and travel to Red Bank Road.	0.7	14.3
Turn LEFT on Red Bank Road and go to the intersection with Baux Mountain Road.	4.8	19.1
Go STRAIGHT on Baux Mountain Road, CROSS Old Hollow Road (N.C. 66) and continue on Baux Mountain Road (road number changes to SR 2211) to Motor Road.	2.3	21.4
Turn RIGHT on Motor Road and go to the stop sign at Indiana Avenue.	2.3	23.7
Turn LEFT on Indiana Avenue and ride to Polo Road.	0.1	23.8
Turn RIGHT on Polo Road and continue to Wingate Road at the entrance to Wake Forest University.	1.4	25.2
Turn LEFT on Wingate Road, then bear RIGHT onto Wake Forest Road, riding around Wait Chapel. Continue on Wake Forest Road as it turns to the right and ride to the three-way stop in front of Salem Hall.	0.6	25.8

Mile-by-Mile Directions	Distance to Next Turn	Total Distance
Turn RIGHT on Wake Forest Road and travel about 50 feet before turning LEFT onto Faculty Drive. You will see the path that leads through stone columns to Reynolda Village and Ken's Bike Shop on the right.	0.1	25.9
Turn RIGHT on the path to Reynolda Village.	0.2	26.1
Turn LEFT at the end of the path and go up the hill to Ken's Bike Shop.	0.1	26.2

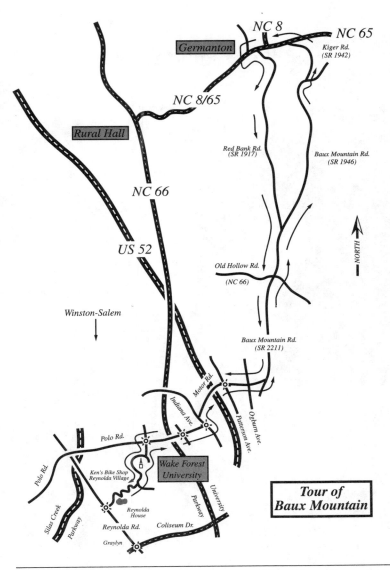

NC 8

NC 65

Germanton

Kiger Rd.
(SR 1942)

NC 8/65

Rural Hall

Red Bank Rd.
(SR 1917)

Baux Mountain Rd.
(SR 1946)

NC 66

NORTH

US 52

Old Hollow Rd.

(NC 66)

Winston-Salem

Baux Mountain Rd.
(SR 2211)

Motor Rd.

Indiana Ave.

Ogburn Ave.

Patterson Ave.

Polo Rd.

Ken's Bike Shop
Reynolda Village

Wake Forest
University

University
Parkway

Polo Rd.

Silas Creek
Parkway

Reynolda
House

Reynolda Rd.

Coliseum Dr.

Graylyn

**Tour of
Baux Mountain**

Tour of Hanging Rock

Description of the route

By far the most difficult ride in this book, this tour offers challenges for even the fittest of riders. Distance is the least of these challenges. After you cross Patterson Avenue, the steep hill

on Motor Road is just a glimpse of what lies ahead. Baux Mountain Road is slightly downhill with curves, then Red Bank Road is level and curvy with a slightly rough surface. N.C. 8/N.C. 65 is busy, but the distance from Buffalo Creek into the town of Germanton is short.

Starting point
   Ken's Bike Shop in Reynolda Village
Distance
   69.5 miles
Terrain
   Very hilly
Food and drinks
   Reynolda Village; the Citgo Station in Quaker Gap; Danbury
Recommendations
   It is best to ride this route later in the season—when you're in shape for it. Don't ride this route during rush hours!

There is a Citgo station on the corner in Quaker Gap for those needing a rest stop. After you cross Town Fork Creek, the roller coaster starts with a 2.5-mile climb. The reward is a curvy downhill, with great vistas of large pastures and surrounding mountains. In the middle of the valley, a sign points to Roger's Arabian Farm on the left. Then it's uphill again. The surface of Mountainview Road is rough in places. The dignified Haw Pond Church stands as a sentinel for riders who pedal past neatly mown yards and acres of burley tobacco.

Don't let the name Flat Shoals Road fool you—there's nothing flat about it. Immediately after your turn onto Flat Shoals Road, there's a country store on the left, if you need to fortify yourself before you climb some more. The community of Quaker Gap takes its name from its location between mountains. The route takes an undulating downhill past a small lake. Hanging Rock looms on the right. Another country store is located 2.1 miles from the last turn in the community of Quaker Gap.

When you reach Moore's Springs Road, look to your left for a great view. You'll pass the Sertoma 4-H Education Center on the left before you enter a gorgeous wooded area. When you cross the bridge on this part of N.C. Bike Route 4, listen for a small waterfall on your right. After you pass the Hanging Rock Outdoor Center, you'll have a fantastic view of Hanging Rock.

As you enter Hanging Rock State Park, get ready for a steady major climb to the top. All around you'll see evidence of a major winter storm that downed many trees and topped others. The visitors center offers great views, as well as exhibits on the Saura Indians who inhabited this area for centuries. On your return, the picturesque town of Danbury, with its architectural gems clinging to the rocky hillsides, has been designated a National Historic District.

As you leave Danbury, you have the option of taking N.C. 8 all the way back to Germanton, or turning right on Mountain Road at mile 41.8. The N.C. 8 option includes fewer climbs, but has much more traffic.

Mile-by-Mile Directions	Distance to Next Turn	Total Distance
From Ken's Bike Shop, take the path from Reynolda Village across Lake Katharine to Wake Forest University.	0.2	0.2
Turn LEFT at the end of the path onto Faculty Drive and go to the stop sign at Wake Forest Road. Turn RIGHT and travel about 50 feet to the three-way stop across from Salem Hall.	0.1	0.3
Turn LEFT on Wake Forest Road and ride through the campus, past Wait Chapel to Wingate Road.	0.4	0.7
Turn LEFT on Wingate Road and go to the signal at Polo Road.	0.2	0.9
Turn RIGHT on Polo Road and travel to the signal at Cherry Street.	0.8	1.7
CROSS Cherry Street and continue on Polo Road to the signal at Indiana Avenue.	0.6	2.3
Turn LEFT on Indiana Avenue and go to Motor Road.	0.2	2.5
Turn RIGHT on Motor Road. CROSS Patterson and Ogburn Avenues and Old Rural Hall Road continuing on Motor Road to the stop sign at Baux Mountain Road.	2.3	4.8
Turn LEFT on Baux Mountain Road (at the city limits, this road becomes SR 2211) and ride to the stop sign at Old Hollow Road (N.C. 66).	2.4	7.2
CROSS Old Hollow Road and continue on Baux Mountain Road (the road number changes to SR 1946) to the fork at Red Bank Road (SR 1917).	1.1	8.3

Mile-by-Mile Directions	Distance to Next Turn	Total Distance
CONTINUE straight onto Red Bank Road. The county bike route goes straight here, but Baux Mountain Road (SR 1946) goes to the right. Stay on Red Bank Road and ride to the stop sign at N.C. 65.	4.8	13.1
Turn LEFT on N.C. 8/N.C. 65 and travel to Friendship Road (SR 1955).	0.3	13.4
Turn RIGHT on Friendship Road, which remains SR 1955, and ride to the stop sign at Quaker Gap community.	5.7	19.1
Turn LEFT on Friendship Road and continue to the stop sign at Mountainview Road (SR 1974).	0.1	19.2
CROSS Mountainview Road on Friendship Road and ride to the stop sign at Flat Shoals Road (SR 2019).	3.3	22.5
Turn LEFT on Flat Shoals Road and go to the stop sign at N.C. 66.	2.6	25.1
Turn RIGHT on N.C. 66 and continue to Moore's Springs Road (SR 1001).	2.7	27.8
Turn RIGHT on Moore's Springs Road and ride to Hanging Rock Park Road (SR 2015-1001).	5.5	33.3
Turn RIGHT on Hanging Rock Park Road and go to the turn into the visitors center.	1.8	35.1
Turn LEFT toward the visitors center, then return to the main road.	0.2	35.3
Turn LEFT at the stop sign and follow the main road to go toward the lake, bathhouse, picnic tables, and restrooms.	0.3	35.6

Mile-by-Mile Directions	Distance to Next Turn	Total Distance
Return to park entrance and gate.	2.1	37.7
CONTINUE straight on Hanging Rock Park Road to the stop sign at N.C. 8.	1.5	39.2
Turn RIGHT on N.C. 8/N.C. 89 and ride to Mountain Road (SR 2018).	2.6	41.8
Turn RIGHT on Mountain Road and travel to Flat Shoals Road.	4.0	45.8
Turn LEFT on Flat Shoals Road and go to Hawkins Road (SR 1973).	1.2	47.0
Turn RIGHT on Hawkins Road and continue to Friendship Road.	3.4	50.4
Turn LEFT on Friendship Road and take an IMMEDIATE RIGHT to stay on Friendship Road to N.C. 8/N.C. 65.	5.7	56.1
Turn LEFT on N.C. 8/N.C. 65 and go to Red Bank Road.	0.3	56.4
Turn RIGHT on Red Bank Road and go to the intersection with Baux Mountain Road at Shiloh Church.	4.8	61.2
CONTINUE straight on Baux Mountain Road to Old Hollow Road.	1.2	62.4
CROSS Old Hollow Road and continue on Baux Mountain Road to Motor Road.	2.4	64.8
Turn RIGHT on Motor Road and go to Indiana Avenue.	2.3	67.1
Turn LEFT on Indiana Avenue and ride to Polo Road.	0.2	67.3

Mile-by-Mile Directions	Distance to Next Turn	Total Distance
Turn RIGHT on Polo Road and continue to Wingate Road at the entrance to Wake Forest University.	1.3	68.6
Turn LEFT at Wingate Road and go to Wake Forest Road.	0.2	68.8
Turn RIGHT on Wake Forest Road. Stay on Wake Forest Road, passing Wait Chapel and curving right to the three-way stop.	0.4	69.2
Turn RIGHT on Wake Forest Road and take a quick LEFT onto Faculty Drive. You will see the path that leads through stone columns to Reynolda Village and Ken's Bike Shop on the right.	0.1	69.3
Turn RIGHT onto the path and ride back to Ken's Bike Shop.	0.2	69.5

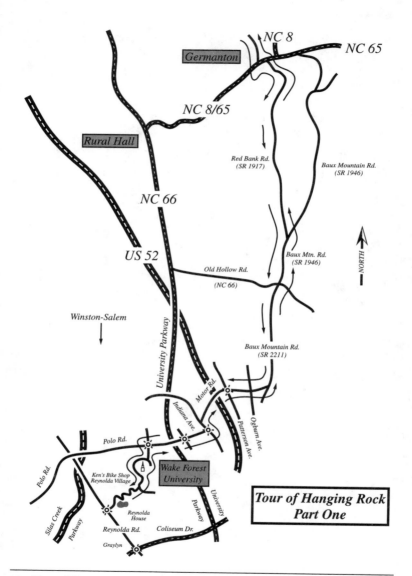

Tour of Hanging Rock
Part One

NC 8

NC 65

Germanton

NC 8/65

Rural Hall

Red Bank Rd.
(SR 1917)

Baux Mountain Rd.
(SR 1946)

NC 66

US 52

NORTH

Baux Mtn. Rd.
(SR 1946)

Old Hollow Rd.

(NC 66)

Winston-Salem

Baux Mountain Rd.
(SR 2211)

University Parkway

Motor Rd.

Ogburn Ave.

Indiana Ave.

Patterson Ave.

Polo Rd.

Ken's Bike Shop
Reynolda Village

Wake Forest
University

University Parkway

Silas Creek

Parkway

Polo Rd.

Reynolda
House

Reynolda Rd.

Coliseum Dr.

Graylyn

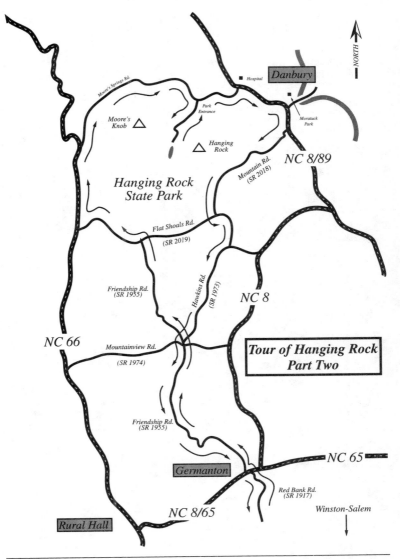

NORTH

Danbury

Hospital

Park Entrance

Moore's Springs Rd.

Moore's Knob △

△ Hanging Rock

Hanging Rock State Park

Moratuck Park

NC 8/89

Mountain Rd. (SR 2018)

Flat Shoals Rd. (SR 2019)

Friendship Rd. (SR 1955)

Hawkins Rd. (SR 1973)

NC 8

NC 66

Mountainview Rd. (SR 1974)

Friendship Rd. (SR 1955)

Tour of Hanging Rock Part Two

NC 65

Germanton

Red Bank Rd. (SR 1917)

Winston-Salem

NC 8/65

Rural Hall

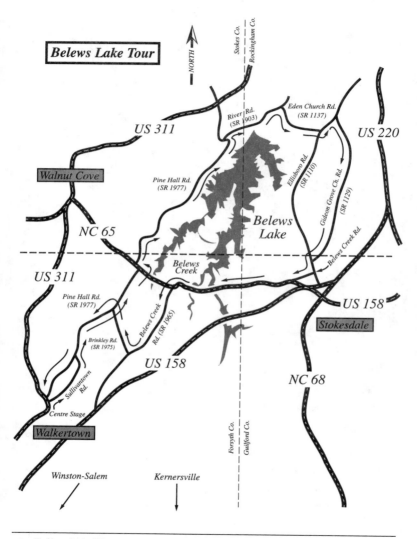

Belews Lake Tour

Description of the route

Mike and Linda Hastings discovered this route and provided the information. It's an unusual route for the Forsyth County area be-

Starting point
Centre Stage Shopping Center in Walkertown

Distance
40.0 miles (The ride is a little shorter if you use the option.)

Terrain
Rolling to hilly

Food and drinks
Centre Stage Shopping Center; small stores on Pine Hall Road, Ellisboro Road, and Gideon Church Road; Hillbilly Hideaway

Recommendations
It is best not to ride this route during rush hours. Traffic is busy on N.C. 65.

cause it circles all of Belews Lake, which is rather expansive. The ride starts in Walkertown at the intersection of N.C. 66/ Old Hollow Road and Main Street. You can park at the Centre Stage Shopping Center. Follow Main Street from the shopping center to the route's first turn. Sullivantown Road is very narrow but level. Older and newer houses are widely spaced along either side of this road.

Pine Hall Road is a curvy country road. On the left, you will see a beautiful Methodist church with unusual shutters that are slanted at the top to match the pointed windows. This road is also part of a county bike route and has a speed limit of 45 miles per hour. At mile 1.9, you'll pass a small store. Pine Hall makes a jog at N.C. 65. Your next turn will be 6.5 miles down the road on the right at River Road. On this road, there's a gradual 0.4-mile climb over smooth pavement into Stokes County. Enjoy the nice views off to your right in this area.

If you're hungry for country-style cooking, you may want to stop at Hillbilly Hideaway. It's great for Sunday breakfasts. The road becomes more curvy and rolling as you pedal toward the Belews Lake Steam Station entrance. The Pine Hall Access Road to the lake, which is just beyond the entrance to the steam station, is open to the public. After traveling 5.5 from the turn onto River Road, you will see Smith's Grocery & Grill on your left. Watch for curvy switchbacks that will take you downhill fast. You'll climb from the stream to the stop sign at Ellisboro Road. At this point, you have a choice of taking a more direct route past Carolina Marina, which has more traffic, or opting for a longer, more scenic route. We recommend taking a bit more time. A lot will depend on what time of day and week you're riding.

When you continue on Ellisboro Road, Rocky's Grocery will be on your right. There's another store at the next turn, which is Gideon Church Road. Except for one good uphill, which passes old tobacco barns and fields, this road is fairly flat with little traffic. On the left, cattle graze peacefully almost in the shadows of several tobacco barns located on the right. It's unusual to see so many of these barns clustered in this manner.

Along Belews Lake Road, you'll be able to see the Belews Lake Steam Plant through the trees on the right. After riding 2.7 miles, you cross back into Forsyth County. After riding 3.6 miles, you'll cross the southern end of the lake. There's another good uphill here. Watch for a beautiful old cemetery after riding about 5 miles. Brinkley Road rolls along on a tar-and-gravel surface. Just after you turn back onto Pine Hall Road, there's a small grocery on the right. Dennis-Walnut Cove Road becomes Main Street as you come back into Walkertown. It leads straight into Centre Stage Shopping Center.

Mile-by-Mile Directions	Distance to Next Turn	Total Distance
Exit Center Stage Shopping Center at the signal next to Hardee's. Go STRAIGHT on Main Street in Walkertown to Sullivantown Road.	0.4	0.4
Turn RIGHT on Sullivantown Road and ride to the stop sign at Pine Hall Road (SR 1977).	1.9	2.3
Turn RIGHT on Pine Hall Road and go to the stop sign at N.C. 65.	4.3	6.6
Turn LEFT on N.C. 65 and continue to Pine Hall Road.	0.2	6.8
Turn RIGHT on Pine Hall Road and go to River Road (SR 1903).	6.5	13.3
Turn RIGHT on River Road and ride to Eden Church Road (SR 1137).	2.5	15.8
Turn RIGHT on Eden Church Road and travel to the stop sign at Ellisboro Road (SR 1110).	1.8	17.6
Turn LEFT on Ellisboro Road and go to Gideon Grove Church Road (SR 1129).	0.8	18.4
Turn RIGHT on Gideon Grove Church Road and ride to Ellisboro Road.	6.2	24.6
Turn LEFT on Ellisboro Road and go to Belews Creek Road (SR 1965).	0.3	24.9
Turn RIGHT on Belews Creek Road and travel to N.C. 65/Belews Creek Road.	0.1	25.0

Mile-by-Mile Directions	Distance to Next Turn	Total Distance
Turn RIGHT on N.C. 65/Belews Creek Road and continue to the intersection where N.C. 65 goes off to the right.	5.2	30.2
CONTINUE on Belews Creek Road and go to Brinkley Road (SR 1975).	3.4	33.6
Turn RIGHT on Brinkley Road and ride to the stop sign at Pine Hall Road.	1.6	35.2
Turn LEFT on Pine Hall Road and travel to Dennis-Walnut Cove Road/Main Street.	4.0	39.2
Turn LEFT on Dennis-Walnut Cove Road/Main Street and go straight into the Centre Stage Shopping Center.	0.8	40.0

Family Rides

Bethabara Greenway Trail (East End)

Description of the route

This wonderful trail is fun for the whole family because it passes through Historic Bethabara. There are lots of opportunities for exploration in the park as well as stone skipping in the adjacent stream. The slight downhill at the beginning gives you an easy start. Then the trail flattens out until it comes to the end of the paved trail at Old Town Drive.

The first part of this trail is the old roadbed for Old Town Road, which was originally a curvy road that connected Indiana Avenue with Bethabara Road, just east of the village. When Old Town Road was straightened, the new road connected with Bethabara Road farther east. The city used the old roadbed for a trail that connected to the existing trail in Bethabara. One driveway crosses the trail, so take care there.

Starting point
The trailhead is located 0.2 mile off Old Town Road. Take Silas Creek Parkway to Bethabara Road and turn northwest on Bethabara Road. Old Town Road is 0.2 mile from Silas Creek Parkway. Park on either side of the street.

Distance
2.6 miles

Terrain
There is a small hill at the beginning, but the remainder of the route is flat.

Food and drinks
None, except water fountains when Bethabara Visitors Center is open

Recommendations
This is a route the whole family can enjoy.

The Bethabara Greenway Trail follows and crosses Minorcas Creek. On your right, you'll see the historic buildings and old fort at Bethabara. At the western end of the settlement, several reconstructed buildings are adjacent to the gardens, which Bethabara rents to citizens who plant and tend them. Only plants that grew here in the eighteenth century are allowed in these gardens, so you won't see any tomatoes.

If you want more exercise, you can walk the unpaved trail that crosses the stream to the left and climbs a steep hill to God's Acre at Bethabara. The Moravians refer to their cemeteries as God's Acre. There's also an exercise course in the adjacent park. Bicycles are allowed only on the paved trail.

When you get to the barricade at Old Town Drive, you can turn around and retrace your route to Old Town Road. Remember you'll have that slight uphill at the end.

Mile-by-Mile Directions	Distance to Next Turn	Total Distance
From the sidewalk on Old Town Road, take the paved trail, which starts at the four square wooden posts. Continue to the bridge.	0.3	0.3
CROSS the bridge and follow the paved trail that curves to the left. Continue to the driveway.	0.3	0.6
CROSS the driveway into the Bethabara Park Nature Preserve if you wish to view Gemeinhaus (the original Moravian church at Bethabara).	0.2	0.8
CONTINUE on the trail until you come to a wooden palisade on the right.	0.2	1.0
CONTINUE on the trail to the area where you will see the gardens and several log structures.	0.2	1.2
CONTINUE to the end of the paved trail at Old Town Drive.	0.1	1.3
TURN AROUND and return along the paved trail to Old Town Road.	1.3	2.6

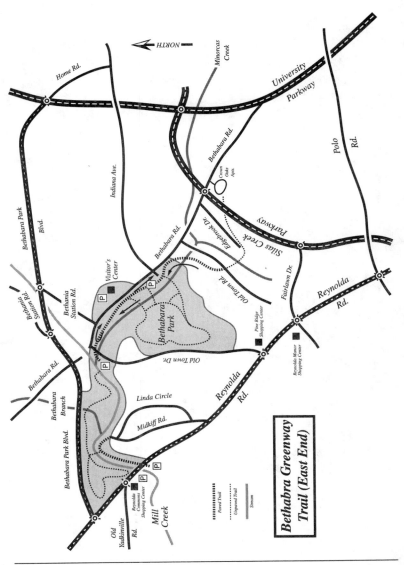

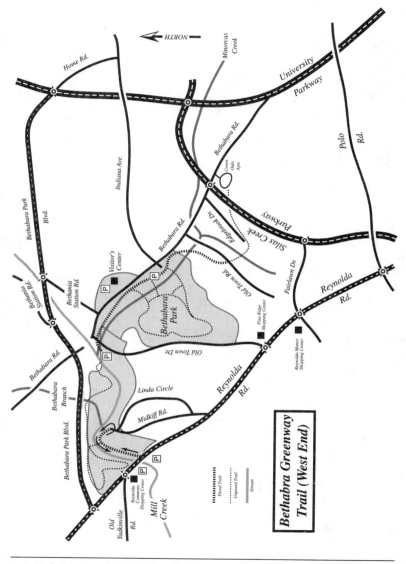

Bethabra Greenway Trail (West End)

NORTH

Home Rd.

Minorcas Creek

University Parkway

Polo Rd.

Bethabara Rd.

Indiana Ave.

Bethabara Park Blvd.

Crown Oaks Apts.

Silas Creek Parkway

Edgebrook Dr.

Old Town Rd.

Fairlawn Dr.

Reynolda Rd.

Bethabara Rd.

Visitor's Center

Bethania Station Rd.

Bethania Station Rd.

Bethabara Park

Pine Ridge Shopping Center

Reynolda Manor Shopping Center

Old Town Dr.

Bethabara Rd.

Bethabara Branch

Linda Circle

Reynolda Rd.

Bethabara Park Blvd.

Midkiff Rd.

Reynolda Commons Shopping Center

Old Yadkinville Rd.

Mill Creek

Paved Trail
Unpaved Trail
Stream

Bethabara Park Trail (West End)

The paved part of the Bethabara Greenway Trail passes through a beautiful wetlands area that Historic Bethabara is working hard to preserve. To begin the ride, you'll exit the Reynolda Commons parking lot and travel on the sidewalk along Reynolda Road. Turn right and head east up the hill. Traffic is heavy along this road, so we recommend walking your bike to the trailhead. There are stairs leading down to the trail or you can go a bit farther and take the paved ramp.

At the bottom of the stairs, the trail curves back to the right and passes under Reynolda Road. The clear water of Mill Creek bounces noisily as it rushes over small rapids under the bridge. As you clear the shadow of the bridge, you'll find yourself in a lovely hardwood forest with the broad stream to your left. At 0.5 mile, a sturdy metal bridge crosses the water to the unpaved

Starting point
Reynolda Commons Shopping Center, located at the intersection of Reynolda Road and Yadkinville Road

Distance
The paved trail is 1.2 miles.

Terrain
Fairly level

Food and drinks
Reynolda Commons Shopping Center

Recommendations
This route is good for children over four years of age. Bikes are allowed on paved trail only.

Mile-by-Mile Directions	Distance to Next Turn	Total Distance
From the trailhead at Reynolda Road, take the paved trail, pass the bridge across Mill Creek and continue to the trail's end at Midkiff Road.	0.6	0.6
Turn around and return to Reynolda Road.	0.6	1.2

walking trails. Because of the fragile nature of the wetland area, bicycles are allowed only on the paved portion of the trail.

The paved trail connects with Midkiff Road in a quiet neighborhood with little motor-vehicle traffic. Midkiff Road connects with Reynolda Road, but you can extend your ride on Linda Circle, which leads to other residential streets. The area is quite hilly, so be prepared to climb if you venture in this direction.

Reynolda Village to Wake Forest

Description of the route

This delightful route follows the paved path through the woods from Reynolda Village to the main campus of Wake Forest University. The path is fairly wide but can be crowded with joggers and walkers, so be careful. Faculty Drive is so named because many professors and staff members live in the houses that line this street adjacent to the campus. Most vehicles here belong to someone associated with the university. When you get to the circle at the end of Faculty Drive, you'll be able to see University Parkway through the trees. A pedestrian gate leads to the sidewalk on University.

From Faculty Drive, the route goes to Royall Drive, which parallels the longer Faculty Drive. From Royall Drive, you will travel briefly on Timberlake Road before returning to Faculty Drive. At the intersection with Timberlake and Faculty, you can go left to return to the path to Reynolda Village or go right and take a longer route through the main part of campus. To go through campus, take Wingate Road from

Starting point
  Ken's Bike Shop in Reynolda Village
Distance
  2.5 miles, with an option of expanding the ride to 4 miles
Terrain
  A few slight hills, but mostly level
Food and drinks
  Restaurants in Reynolda Village; Benson University Center on the Wake Forest University campus
Recommendations
  At certain times, traffic is busy on the main part of campus; there is usually little traffic on Sunday afternoons.

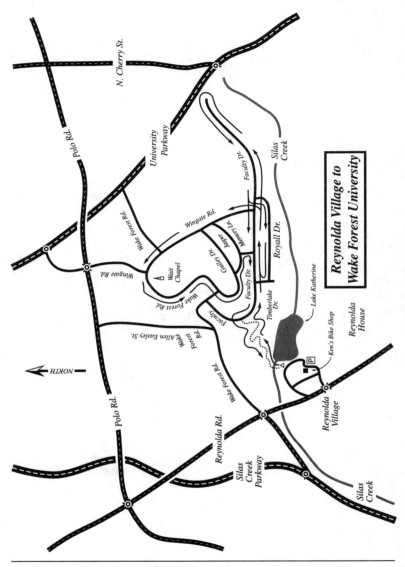

Reynolda Village to Wake Forest University

NORTH

N. Cherry St.

Polo Rd.

University Parkway

Wake Forest Rd.

Wingate Rd.

Wingate Rd.

Faculty Dr.

Silas Creek

Royall Dr.

Memory Ln.

Griffin Dr.

Wait Chapel

Wake Forest Rd.

Faculty Dr.

Faculty Dr.

Timberlake Dr.

Lake Katherine

Ken's Bike Shop

Reynolda House

Wake Forest Rd.

Allen Easley St.

Reynolda Village

Reynolda Rd.

Silas Creek Parkway

Silas Creek

Polo Rd.

Faculty Drive to Wake Forest Road, which is the main route through campus. On your right as you ride through campus, you'll pass the practice fields. You will then pass the gymnasium on the right and the Calloway School of Business and Accountancy on the left.

Next, you will see the men's dormitories, located around a quadrangle. As you round a curve on Wake Forest Road, you'll pass the back of Wait Chapel, whose tall spire is a major landmark in Winston-Salem. As you follow the road that curves behind the chapel, the road will straighten. You'll see the Z. Smith Reynolds Library straight ahead and the Benson University Center on the left. Wake Forest Road curves to the right before reaching a three-way stop. After the stop sign, you'll travel between various science buildings before turning back toward Faculty Drive.

Mile-by-Mile Directions	Distance to Next Turn	Total Distance
From Ken's Bike Shop, take the hill down toward Lake Katherine and bear LEFT.	0.1	0.1
Take a right onto the path that crosses the lake. This path leads from Reynolda Village to Wake Forest University.	0.2	0.3
Go RIGHT onto Faculty Drive at the end of the path. Go to the end of Faculty Drive and go around the circle there.	1.0	1.3
CONTINUE on Faculty Drive to Royall Drive.	0.3	1.6
Turn LEFT on Royall Drive and go to the stop sign at Timberlake Road.	0.4	2.0
Turn RIGHT on Timberlake Road and go to the stop sign at Faculty Drive.	0.1	2.1
Turn LEFT on Faculty Drive and go to the path that leads to Reynolda Village the same way you came in.	0.1	2.2

Mile-by-Mile Directions	Distance to Next Turn	Total Distance
Option: From the intersection of Timberlake Road and Faculty Drive, turn RIGHT on Faculty Drive and ride to Wingate Road.	0.3	2.5
Turn LEFT on Wingate Road, which becomes Wake Forest Road after Wingate goes off to the right. Stay on Wake Forest Road, circling Wait Chapel. You will follow Wake Forest Road as it turns to the right and continue to the three-way stop sign at Salem Hall.	0.9	3.4
Go STRAIGHT at the three-way stop to Jasper Memory Lane. Continue on Jasper Memory Lane until you reach the stop sign at Faculty Drive.	0.2	3.6
Turn RIGHT on Faculty Drive and ride to the path on the left, which leads to Reynolda Village.	0.2	3.8
Turn LEFT on the path leading to Reynolda Village.	0.3	4.1

Silas Creek Greenway

Starting point
Shaffner Park on Yorkshire Road, near Silas Creek Parkway

Distance
1.6 miles

Terrain
Flat

Food and drinks
Water fountains at the park

Recommendations
This is an excellent route for young children who are learning to ride.

Description of the route

This short but scenic greenway connects Yorkshire Road to Robinhood Road and parallels Silas Creek Parkway. Because of this trail's short length, it is not as popular with in-line skaters as other greenways are. However, you're likely to encounter some walkers. The path is eight feet wide, allowing plenty of space for two-way traffic.

It's hard to believe the variety of wildflowers and berries that thrive this close to the busy parkway. In summer, kudzu abounds, hiding wonderful purple flowers under its dark green foliage. Wild blackberries are available for picking in late July to early August.

The best part of this trail is its flatness, which makes it ideal for 4- to 7-year-old children who are learning to bicycle and need space to practice safely.

Mile-by-Mile Directions	Distance to Next Turn	Total Distance
From the parking lot at Shaffner Park, CROSS Yorkshire Road very carefully to the greenway.	0.8	0.8
Turn around and retrace your route on the greenway to Yorkshire Road.	0.8	1.6

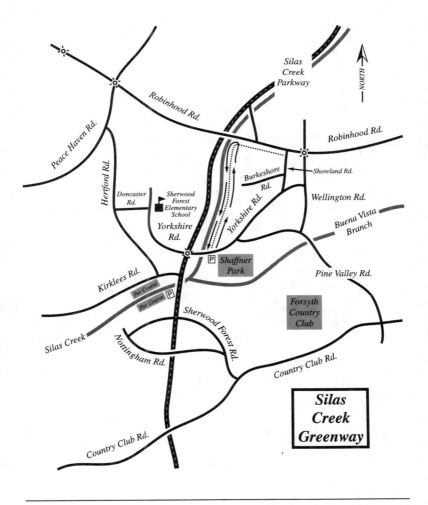

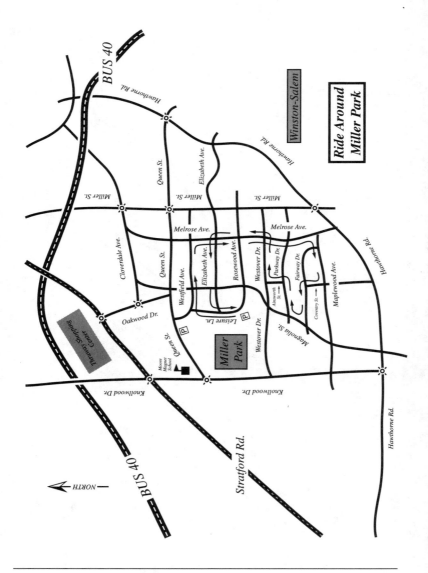

Ride Around Miller Park

Description of the route

Parents looking for a good ride for young children should try this route. The entire route is on residential streets in Ardmore, one of Winston-Salem's lovely old neighborhoods that dates to the 1930s and 40s. Although Ardmore's trees were devastated when a tornado touched down in 1989, more were planted. These younger tress joined those that survived not only the tornado but also Hurricane Hugo later that year.

These streets wander through Ardmore from a starting point at Miller Park. The route does not cross any major streets and carefully avoids busy streets.

Most of these streets are level, although there is a slight incline as you head away from the park and return on Melrose Street. For

Starting point

Parking lot on Leisure Lane. To reach the parking lot from Business 40, take the Knollwood Street Exit. Take Knollwood Street south to Queen Street. Turn left on Queen Street and go to Westfield Avenue. Turn right on Westfield Avenue and then right onto Leisure Lane. The parking lot is a little over 0.1 mile from your turn onto Leisure Lane. Parking is also available on the street.

Distance

2.6 miles

Terrain

Mostly flat, with a couple of slight hills

Food and drinks

Water fountains in Miller Park

Recommendations

This ride is ideal for families with children, ages seven and older.

Mile-by-Mile Directions	Distance to Next Turn	Total Distance
From the parking lot, turn LEFT on Leisure Lane and go to the stop sign at Westfield Avenue.	0.1	0.1
Turn RIGHT on Westfield Avenue and ride two blocks to the stop sign at Melrose Street.	0.5	0.6
Turn RIGHT on Melrose Street and ride five blocks to Maplewood Avenue. Note that Maplewood zigzags at this juncture, so you will see Maplewood Avenue on your left before you reach the section where you turn.	0.5	1.1
Turn RIGHT on Maplewood Avenue and ride two blocks to Coventry Street.	0.2	1.3
Turn RIGHT on Coventry Street and ride one block to Fairway Drive. Turn left on Fairway Drive and go one block to a stop sign at Magnolia Street.	0.1	1.4
Turn RIGHT on Magnolia Street and ride one block to Parkway Drive.	0.1	1.5
Turn RIGHT on Parkway Drive and go one block to Ainsworth Street. Turn LEFT on Ainsworth Street and go to the stop sign at Westover Drive.	0.1	1.6
Go RIGHT on Westover Drive and go one block to the four-way stop sign at Melrose Street.	0.5	2.1
Turn LEFT on Melrose Street and ride two blocks to Elizabeth Avenue.	0.2	2.3
Turn LEFT on Elizabeth Avenue and go two blocks to the stop sign at Leisure Street.	0.1	2.4

children younger than five years of age, Miller Park has paved trails and parking lots, which can allow them to practice their bike-handling skills without worrying about cars. The park has restrooms and water fountains.

Mile-by-Mile Directions	Distance to Next Turn	Total Distance
Turn LEFT on Leisure Lane and go less than one block to the parking lot on the right at Miller Park.	0.1	2.5

Option:
To ride the closest trail through the park, start at the trailhead to the left of the building where the restrooms are housed on the west side of the Leisure Lane parking lot. Take the first left toward the playground. The trail curves downhill and follows the stream toward the north, passing three picnic shelters on the left. This trail is the most level one in this part of the park, although connecting trails can be a little hilly.

Downtown Strollway

Description of the route

From the entrance on Fourth Street, follow the strollway south toward Old Salem. Take care when crossing Third, Second, and First Streets and Brookstown Avenue. A sidewalk connects the strollway between Third and Second Streets. Between Second and First Streets, you'll pass Corpening Plaza, where you may want to wander around the fountains. They provide a pleasant spray on windy days in the spring and summer.

The strollway winds south of First Street. You'll pass under Business 40 and pass the U.S. Bankruptcy Court building. Beyond that, the trail parallels Old Salem Road. At the intersection with Academy Street, you can use the sidewalk and the traffic signal to cross Old Salem Road to Old Salem. The visitors center is on your right after you cross Old Salem Road. Mayberry's Restaurant offers ice

Starting point

The entrance to the strollway is on West Fourth Street, between Trade and Cherry Streets, in downtown Winston-Salem. Parking is available in the parking deck on Cherry Street, between Fourth and Fifth Streets. There is also some on-street parking.

Distance

2.06 miles roundtrip

Terrain

Downhill to Old Salem; a gradual uphill on the return

Food and drinks

Restaurants on Fourth Street during the week; Mayberry's in Old Salem during the day and Darryl's on Brookstown Avenue.

Recommendations

This ride is good for children six years of age or older.

Mile-by-Mile Directions	Distance to Next Turn	Total Distance
From the entrance at Fourth Street, ride south one block and cross Third Street onto Town Run Lane. Continue to the stop sign at Second Street.	0.14	0.14
CROSS Second Street. Go through the barrier posts and pass One Triad Park (an office building) on the left and the Wachovia Park Building on the right. Continue one block to First Street.	1 block	0.14
CROSS First Street and enter the Strollway, which is indicated by banners on the light poles along the path.	1 block	0.15
PASS through a nicely landscaped area and go under the Business 40 bridge.	0.13	0.28
CONTINUE past the U.S. Bankruptcy Court, Downtown Middle School, the old Southern Railway Building, and underneath the porch of Salem Tower to Brookstown Avenue.	0.14	0.42
CROSS Brookstown Avenue. Pass the historic Brookstown Mill on your right and the Leinbach House on the left on the way to Academy Street.	0.23	0.65
CROSS Academy Street (Old Salem is to the left) and continue to Walnut Street.	0.26	0.91
CROSS Walnut Street and pass under the timbered pedestrian bridge that crosses over to Old Salem.	0.05	0.96
CONTINUE on the trail until it forks just before Salem Avenue. You can turn around or go left or right to connect with the Salem Creek Greenway.	0.07	1.03
RETURN to Fourth Street along the same trail.	1.03	2.06

cream, drinks, or lunch, depending on how hungry you are.

The strollway continues to Salem Avenue, where you can connect with the Salem Creek Greenway. At this point, the greenway uses the south sidewalk along Salem Avenue. You can identify this part of the greenway by the pebble surface. To reach the eastern end of the greenway, turn left on Salem Avenue. If you go to the left along Salem Avenue to Happy Hills Park, you'll see the paved trail that leads to Salem Lake. If you go to the right, the greenway takes you to Marketplace Mall. If you go to the right to Broad Street, you can pick up the trail just south of the intersection with Salem Avenue. This part of the trail takes you to Marketplace Mall. You can also turn around at Salem Avenue and ride back uphill to Fourth Street. Because of this climb, this trail is better for children six years of age and older.

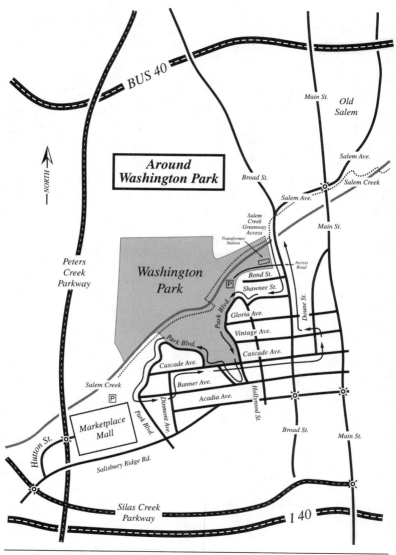

Around Washington Park

Around Washington Park

Description of the route

Despite the big hill at the beginning, this is a delightful ride through one of Winston-Salem's oldest and most charming neighborhoods. If you or your children are daunted by the Broad Street hill, you can walk your bikes up the sidewalk to Shawnee Street or park on Shawnee and start from there. Except for Broad Street, this route follows neighborhood streets with little to no traffic.

Park Boulevard takes its name from its location at the perimeter of Washington Park. The homes along this quiet and lovely street overlook the vast expanse of the park. The neighborhood, which is undergoing a resurgence, mixes large and small homes in an interesting fashion. Take care when you turn left on Cascade Avenue at the end of the first mile. A large magnolia blocks the view to the left. After you cross Cascade, you'll see a large mansion and estate perched on

Starting point
The Washington Park parking lot is off Broad Street, just south of Salem Avenue. You can also continue from the Salem Creek Greenway at Broad Street.

Distance
2.3 or 2.6 miles, depending on starting point

Terrain
Hilly on Broad Street, otherwise mostly level

Food and drinks
Convenience store at bottom of Broad Street at Salem Avenue

Recommendations
This ride is good for families with children seven years of age and older.

the hilltop to your left. As you pedal away from the park, houses will appear on your right as well. Their position below street level emphasizes the slope of the hills.

There's a slight uphill on Banner Avenue as you go to Dinmont Street. The homes grow larger here. On the final portion of Cascade Avenue, the smaller houses give way to grander, older homes reminiscent of another era. As you approach Broad Street, newer homes on the left are designed to blend unobtrusively with the rest of the neighborhood. When you turn left on Doune Street, you'll face a great view of the Winston-Salem skyline.

Mile-by-Mile Directions	Distance to Next Turn	Total Distance
From Salem Creek Greenway, turn RIGHT on Broad Street to Washington Park entrance.	0.3	0.3
CONTINUE on Broad Street to Shawnee Street.	0.1	0.4
Go RIGHT on Shawnee Street to the stop sign at Park Boulevard.	0.1	0.5
Go RIGHT on Park Boulevard to the stop sign at Cascade Avenue. CROSS Cascade Avenue to the stop sign at Banner Avenue.	0.4	0.9
Turn RIGHT on Banner Avenue, followed by a RIGHT turn on Park Boulevard. Travel on Park Boulevard to the stop sign at Cascade Avenue.	0.1	1.0
Turn LEFT on Cascade Avenue, then make a RIGHT turn on Park Boulevard. Travel on Park Boulevard to Banner Avenue.	0.4	1.4
Turn LEFT on Banner Avenue and travel to Dinmont Street.	0.1	1.5
Turn LEFT on Dinmont Street and travel to the stop sign at Cascade Avenue.	0.1	1.6

Mile-by-Mile Directions	Distance to Next Turn	Total Distance
Turn RIGHT on Cascade Avenue. CROSS Broad Street to the stop sign at Doune Street.	0.4	2.0
Turn LEFT on Doune Street and travel to Vintage Avenue.	0.1	2.1
Turn LEFT on Vintage Avenue and travel to the stop sign at Broad Street.	0.1	2.2
Turn RIGHT on Broad Street and travel to the entrance to Washington Park. Take a LEFT into Washington Park.	0.1	2.3
If you started at the Salem Creek Greenway, continue on Broad Street until you reach the greenway. Take a LEFT onto the greenway.	0.3	2.6

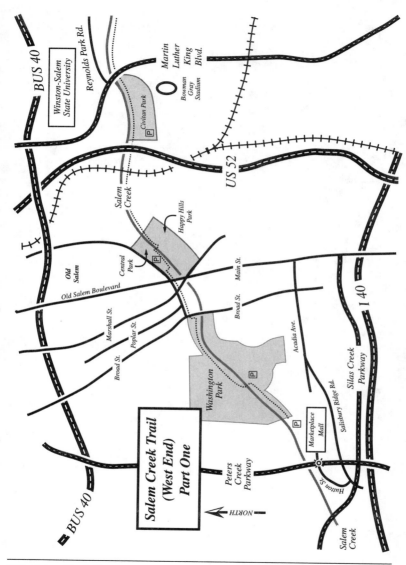

Salem Creek Greenway

Description of the route

This trail, Winston-Salem's first greenway, connects several parks, Old Salem, Salem College, Winston-Salem State University, and Salem Lake Park. Except for the portion between Broad Street and Central Park, which is on a sidewalk, the trail is a paved, eight-foot-wide smooth surface that is pleasant to ride. It's primarily flat but has some up-and-down sections when it crosses under U. S. 52 and travels through Reynolds Park.

Starting point

You can park in the parking lot at Marketplace Mall, located on Peters Creek Parkway, between Business 40 and Silas Creek Parkway. The trailhead is behind the mall, on the northern side.

Distance

9 miles

Terrain

Flat to rolling

Food and drinks

Inside Marketplace Mall; Mayberry's in Old Salem; vending machines at Salem Lake

Recommendations

Be sure to lock your car if you park it at the mall. Ride the greenway with a partner.

From Marketplace Mall, you'll pass through Washington Park to Broad Street. At this point, the trail uses the sidewalk instead of following the creek. The first greenway committee for the city had to struggle with the configuration of this part of the trail. Between Broad and Main Streets, the creek banks are very steep, and businesses on either side use the space all the way to the creek bank. The committee decided that it would be less expensive and more practical to use sidewalks through this section. The sidewalks that are part of the trail have a pebble

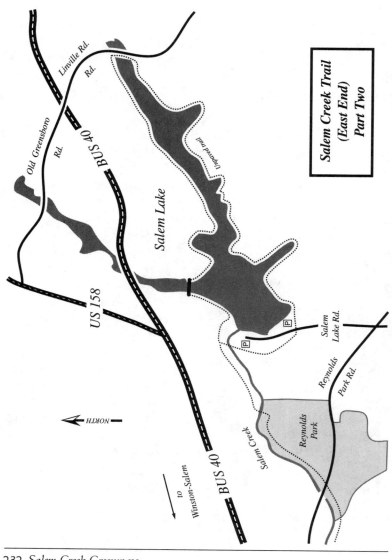

Salem Creek Trail
(East End)
Part Two

Linville Rd.

Rd.

Old Greensboro

Rd.

BUS 40

unpaved trail

Salem Lake

US 158

P

P

Salem Lake Rd.

Reynolds

Park Rd.

NORTH

Reynolds
Park

to
Winston-Salem

BUS 40

Salem Creek

coating to distinguish them from regular sidewalks.

When you cross Old Salem Road, you have the option of crossing Salem Avenue and following Old Main Street through the southern end of Old Salem. Riding through the village by bike is wonderful and really allows you to take in the sights. Where you pick up the trail again in Central Park, you'll pass through Happy Hills Park, under U. S. 52 and Vargrave Street, then past the Anderson Center and Winston-Salem State University. After you cross under Reynolds Park Road, you'll skirt the edge of Reynolds Park Golf Course.

The section between Marketplace Mall and Broad Street is good for younger children, although there can be a lot of in-line skaters and pedestrians. In the section between Old Salem Road and Salem Lake, there are a few places where the trail passes through culverts. In these sections, the narrow pavement has a drop-off, so take special care. The area under Reynolds Park Road sometimes floods and can be muddy after a heavy rain.

At Salem Lake, you have the option of taking the unpaved Salem Lake Trail, which hugs the lake edge. This trail is recommended only for mountain bikes or those with larger tires that can handle the rougher surface.

Mile-by-Mile Directions	Distance to Next Turn	Total Distance
From Marketplace Mall, travel LEFT on the greenway through Washington Park to Broad Street.	1.0	1.0
Turn LEFT onto Broad and take an almost immediate RIGHT onto Salem Avenue. At this point, the greenway uses the south sidewalk along Salem Avenue. You can identify this part of the greenway by the pebble surface. You'll see signs for continuation of the greenway on your right about 100 feet from the intersection with Old Salem Road.	1.0	2.0

Mile-by-Mile Directions	Distance to Next Turn	Total Distance
Turn RIGHT onto the paved trail and travel until you come to a bridge on the left. CROSS the bridge and continue through Happy Hills Park to Salem Lake.	2.5 miles	4.5
TURN AROUND and return to Marketplace Mall.	4.5	9.0

Bowen Branch Trail

Description of the route

This short, 12-foot-wide paved trail is on the banks of Brushy Fork Creek between New Walkertown Road and Bowen Boulevard. Eventually the city plans to connect this trail with the Brushy Fork Greenway and a connector to Liberty Street. For now, it offers a short but safe off-street route that is good for children who are under ten years of age. The trail itself is only 0.3 mile long, but it does connect with a sidewalk on the south side of Bowen Boulevard. You can extend the ride by traveling on this sidewalk for the short distance to Bowen Boulevard Park & Fitness Center, which is just beyond the intersection with Attucks Street. This park backs up to Ashley Middle School. At Attucks Street, you can pick up Forsyth County Bike Routes 11 and 7.

Starting point

The greenway starts off Bowen Boulevard, where it crosses Brushy Fork Creek. Bowen Boulevard is located off U.S. 311 (New Walkertown Road) in northeast Winston-Salem. Bowen Boulevard is just north of Waterworks Road, where you will see signs directing you to the Winston Lake Family YMCA.

Distance

0.6 mile

Terrain

Level

Food and drinks

Stores along New Walkertown Road

Recommendations

Traffic is busy on New Walkertown Road, so take care crossing there if you want to reach the sites on the other side.

Mile-by-Mile Directions	Distance to Next Turn	Total Distance
From the trailhead at Bowen Boulevard, ride on the trail toward New Walkertown Road (U. S. 311) where you turn around.	0.3	0.3
From New Walkertown Road, return to Bowen Boulevard.	0.3	0.6

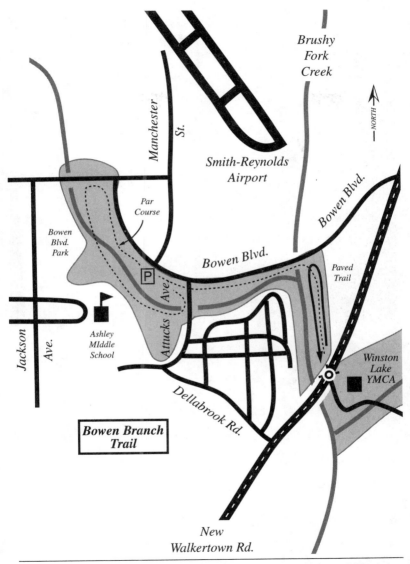

Brushy Fork Creek

NORTH

Manchester St.

Smith-Reynolds Airport

Par Course

Bowen Blvd. Park

Bowen Blvd.

Bowen Blvd.

Paved Trail

P

Attucks Ave.

Jackson Ave.

Ashley MIddle School

Dellabrook Rd.

Winston Lake YMCA

Bowen Branch Trail

New Walkertown Rd.

Mountain Bike Trails

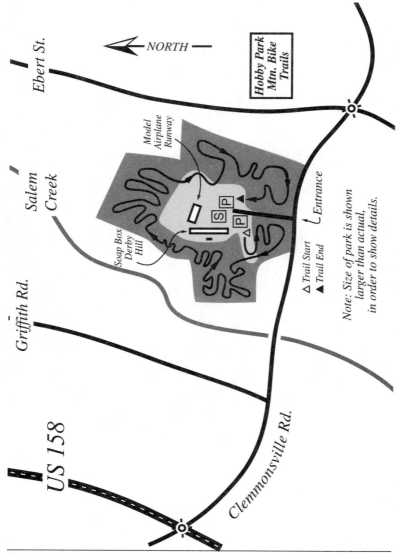

NORTH

Ebert St.

Hobby Park
Mtn. Bike
Trails

Model
Airplane
Runway

Salem
Creek

Soap Box
Derby Hill

S P

P

Entrance

△ Trail Start
▲ Trail End

Note: Size of park is shown
larger than actual,
in order to show details.

Griffith Rd.

US 158

Clemmonsville Rd.

Hobby Park

Description of the route

Hobby Park is Winston-Salem's first real mountain-bike park. To reach the park from Silas Creek Parkway, take Ebert Street south to the first stoplight, which is Clemmonsville Road. Take a right onto Clemmonsville

Starting point

The entrance to Hobby Park is off Clemmonsville Road between Ebert Street and Stratford Road.

Distance

Approximately 7 miles

Terrain

Rugged

Food and drinks

Convenience store located at the intersection of Ebert Street and Clemmonsville Road, which is about 1 mile from the park

Recommendations

Only moderately to very experienced riders should try this route.

Road and travel a half mile to the entrance of Hobby Park.

Hobby Park is a large park adjacent to the old town dump, which explains the park's own special smells. As you come into the park, there is a small parking lot on the left. This is the best place to park if you are mountain biking. If you go straight, you will see the city's Soap Box Derby hill on the left. You will eventually come to a lower parking lot, which has a shelter. This lot is next to a large field that has a landing strip for model airplanes.

The mountain-bike trailhead is marked by a large bulletin board, which is located to the left of the upper parking lot. Riders should note that this course is for intermediate and advanced riders only. A beginner should be able to easily ride the Tanglewood mountain-bike routes before trying Hobby Park.

The beginning of the Hobby Park course is difficult, with rocks and drop offs. It then has sharp climbs and steep descents for a few miles as the course curves alongside the Soap Box Derby hill. Some of the hills on this route may be too steep to climb, so you may need to push your bike.

You will then go around a lake, up a hill, and around another lake to a section with a gully. This section has large rocks and drop offs. It is probably the most technically difficult area in the park.

The route then rides alongside a fence until you reach a creek crossing, which usually has an interesting smell. You should stay right at this crossing.

Go up a hill and make a left into a field. Go around the field and ride back into the woods. Follow the single track. As you come out of the woods, stay to the left.

Go straight uphill on the single track as it travels alongside Clemmonsville Road. There is an off-camber downhill, followed by an off-camber climb. As you leave the woods, you will see the parking lot on the left.

Volunteers maintain this course, so you may find bridges out or other hazards. Be careful! There is no medical help close to this course. We encourage you to ride with a friend, so you can take care of each other.

Because the course was built on the site of an old garbage dump, the course drains very well. It dries quickly, so you can usually ride within one or two days after a hard rain. You should not ride the trails while they're wet because it causes erosion. Help maintain these trails so we can continue to use them.

The park is open from sunrise to 10:30 P.M.

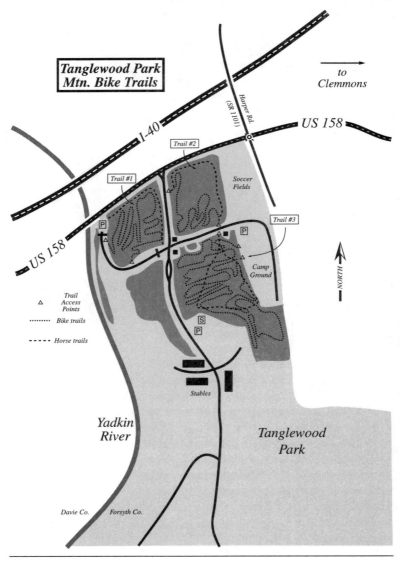

Tanglewood Park Mtn. Bike Trails

to Clemmons

I-40

Harper Rd. (SR 1101)

US 158

US 158

Trail #1

Trail #2

Trail #3

Soccer Fields

Camp Ground

NORTH

△ Trail Access Points

.... Bike trails

----- Horse trails

S

P

P

P

P

Stables

Yadkin River

Tanglewood Park

Davie Co.   Forsyth Co.

Tanglewood Trails

Note: At the time of this book's publication, Tanglewood officials are re-examining the trail configuration in an effort to accommodate pedestrians, equestrians, and cyclists compatibly. Please check with the front gate to learn which trails are still open for mountain bikers.

Trail 1

Starting point

The trailhead is best accessed at the gravel parking lot just before the Katherine Crosby Bridge crosses the Yadkin on U.S. 158. Go past the metal gate, toward the concert shell. The path goes into the woods twenty to thirty feet from the road.

Distance

2 miles

Terrain

Rolling, but no hills; rough terrain

Recommendations

This is the best Tanglewood trail for beginning mountain bikers, but make sure you know how to handle the bike. The trail uses as much of the land as possible. There are a lot of tight turns, roots and small logs. You will need to be able to pick up your front wheel to ride over the roots and logs comfortably. After traveling 1.75 miles, the trail comes out on the horse trail. Proceed across a small bridge. The bike trail turns immediately into the woods. After 0.25 mile, this section comes out on the gravel road about 100 yards below the trailhead. Turn right out of the woods onto the gravel road to return to the parking lot.

Trail 2
Starting point
There is no parking area at the trailhead, so you should park at the welcome center or near the soccer fields and ride on the road to the trailhead. To get to the trailhead from the Welcome Center, take the main park road back toward the U.S. 158 entrance. About 200 feet before the park road intersects with U.S. 158, take a right onto the horse trail.

Distance
1 mile

Terrain
Some hills; rough terrain

Recommendations
Compared to the other two trails, this trail has a moderate level of difficulty. Be sure to yield to walkers and horses on this trail. From the trailhead at the horse trail, travel 100 feet to a path that goes off to the right. Turn right and follow the winding path. This section is more difficult than Trail 1 because it has short, steep climbs and more objects to overcome. You will cross the horse trail at least 2 times. Always remember to go straight across these intersections. The trail ends at the horse trail, which is located just across the park road from the brown ranger's house. This house is located between the soccer fields and the welcome center.

Thanks to local cyclists, Tanglewood Park, Forsyth County's premier park, now has mountain-bike trails. The plan for the trails was hatched when Bob Golf, the park superintendent at the time, met with a local cyclist to discuss possible uses for some back areas of the park. They all agreed that mountain-bike trails would be a good way to use park land. Volunteers installed the trails during the winters of 1998 and 1999 and continue to work on the trails regularly.

The trails are carefully laid out to avoid the horse trails as much as possible. Although the bike trails gain access from the horse trails in a few areas, the bike trails are designed to meet the horse trails at distinct intersections where the mountain-bike trail always goes straight across the horse trail. There is little horse traffic in these areas, but it is imperative that mountain bikers stay off the horse trails. When you approach horses at an intersection or trail access, you should stop and let the horse pass before continuing. Horses are sometimes easily spooked and can throw a rider, potentially causing serious injury. Please also carry out all of your trash.

Trail 3

Starting point

The parking areas are between the Welcome Center, campgrounds and Shelter #2. The easiest access to the trail is through the field across from the soccer field or from the horse trail that runs beside the brown ranger's house, located near the soccer field.

Distance

4.6 miles

Terrain

Hilly, with rough terrain

Recommendations

This trail is best for moderate-to-experienced mountain bikers. This is the longest and most difficult of Tanglewood's mountain-bike trails. After entering the trailhead on the horse trail, go about 100 feet. You will see the mountain-bike path off to your right. This trail goes through the woods behind the Welcome Center and meanders over creeks and up small hills behind Shelter #2 before turning back and passing the former campground area. It eventually comes out at the trailhead across from the soccer fields. You can get lost if you do not always go straight across when intersecting horse trails.

You may often encounter detours on this trail as volunteers work to combat erosion and make trail improvements. Because volunteers maintain the trail there is no structure to changes that are made. Riders should realize that dangerous sections could occur at any point, so you need to dismount your bike and walk whenever you feel your skill level may not be up to the challenge.

The Tanglewood courses are good for beginning-to-advanced riders. Beginners will find Trail #1 the easiest because it has no hills. You can get off your bike where obstacles are too difficult. The other two trails are increasingly difficult, but neither is considered an advanced trail. You will encounter downed trees, tree roots, rocks, ditches, and muddy or sandy areas. This course drains well but should not be ridden when conditions are muddy because of trail erosion. Be careful, and always ride with a buddy who can go for help in case of an injury.

Tanglewood Park is now under the jurisdiction of the Forsyth County Recreation Department, which now oversees the maintenance of the trail system.

Salem Lake

Description of the route

Salem Lake Park is part of the City of Winston-Salem Recreation and Parks Department. It offers the most scenic mountain biking in Forsyth County because the dirt trail circles Salem Lake. The two-directional trail, which is shared by runners, horseback riders, and walkers, is a great place for casual riding for individuals and families.

There are three different access points to the Salem Lake Trail. If you drive into the park via Salem Lake Road, you can park in the lot just before entering the marina. The trailhead starts at the east end of the lot, near the picnic tables. If you go in this direction, you will ride the route counterclockwise.

If you cycle to Salem Lake by way of the Salem Creek Greenway, it's easiest to go straight across the bridge and ride the trail clockwise. The

Starting points
1) The parking lot at the southwest end of Salem Lake. This lot is accessible via Salem Lake Road.
2) From the Salem Creek Greenway, which is covered in the "Family Rides" section. The greenway connects to the Salem Lake Trail.
3) The parking lot at the end of the access road (New Greensboro Road, SR 3300), directly across from the eastbound entrance ramp to Business 40 at Linville Road.

Distance
6.9 miles

Terrain
Mostly flat

Food and drinks
Vending machines or a small concession stand at the park

Recommendations
This route is great for beginning riders and families.

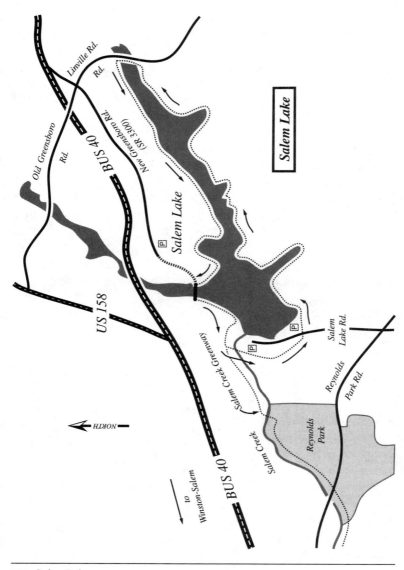

Salem Lake

NORTH

most common access for mountain bikers is from Linville Road and the New Greensboro Road access, where the city built a parking lot for the cyclists. From this access point, you can easily ride in either direction. Please note that at the west end of the lake, the trail travels up the hill as it goes outside the fenced area to connect with the Salem Creek Greenway and/or the trail on the north side of the lake. If you ride the route around the lake clockwise, always keep the lake to your right whenever you have a question about the route. If you ride counterclockwise, always keep the lake to your left.

The trail around Salem Lake is primarily gravel with occasional sandy spots. Gravel areas may be loose or thick with small gravel. You should be aware that next to the dam, the spillway may be flooded. If so, you will have to portage your bike along the side. You should also know that the section of the trail next to Linville Road requires you to ride or walk your bike on a single track that travels alongside the guardrail next to the road.

Because this is a shared-use trail, it's important to watch for other users and exercise your common sense. Sometimes careless riders will race around the lake and create a hazardous situation. For the most part, different users are considerate of each other.

Salem Lake is one of Winston-Salem's principal water supplies, so it's important for cyclists to stay on the trail and not cause erosion along the lake. We encourage all mountain bikers to ride responsibly, so we can all continue to enjoy this wonderful trail.

Mile-by-Mile Directions	Distance to Next Turn	Total Distance
If biking the route counterclockwise, begin on the right (northeast) side of the parking lot on a wide service road.	0.9	0.9
CROSS a cement bridge.	1.8	2.7
CROSS a causeway.	0.7	3.4
Arrive at Linville Road (SR 2662). To the left, it is 0.7 mile to Business 40, Exit 10. Continue on the trail by riding on the single track that parallels the road and re-entering the woods	0.5	3.9
Follow the service road under a power line.	2.1	6.0
You will reach a junction to the left with a causeway and an arched bridge over the lake. To the right is a gravel service road that leads 0.3 mile to a gate and parking lot at the end of New Greensboro Road. It goes 1.2 miles east to Linville Road and its junction with Business 40 at Exit 10. CROSS the bridge.	0.5	6.5
Ride along the shoreline and descend to the base of the dam at a junction with Salem Creek Trail. This is the spillway that may need portage.	0.4	6.9
CROSS the dam and ascend to a gate and the west end of the parking lot; if the gate is locked, follow the paved trail around the fence to the point of origin.		

Appendix

List of Routes by Mileage

Bowen Branch Trail (about 0.6 miles)
Tanglewood Trails (1, 2, and 4.6 miles)
Bethabara Greenway Trail (West End) (1.2)
Silas Creek Greenway (1.6 miles)
Downtown Strollway (2.06 miles)
Around Washington Park (2.3 or 2.6 miles)
Reynolda Village to Wake Forest (2.5 miles + 4-mile option)
Bethabara Greenway Trail (East End) (2.6 miles)
Ride Around Miller Park (2.6 miles)
Salem Lake (6.9 miles)
Hobby Park (7 miles)
Thursday Night Training Ride (8.4 miles)
Salem Creek Greenway (9 miles)
Williams Road Loop (12.9 miles)
Lasater Mill Loop (13.0 miles)
River Ridge Ride (13.4 miles)
Inside Loop (13.5 miles)
Meadowlark Loop (17.4 miles)
Bruce's Lewisville to Tanglewood Ride (18.2 miles)
Chicken Coop Ride (21.7 miles)
Baltimore Road Loop (23.0 miles)

Randy Shields' Training Ride (23.0 miles)
East Bend Out & Back (23.4 miles)
Duffy Loop (24.8 miles)
Tour of Baux Mountain (26.2 miles)
Biathlon Time Trial Route (26.4 miles)
Old Biathlon Loop (26.7 miles)
Shacktown Falls (27.8 miles)
601 Out & Back (28.8 miles)
Bunny Rabbit Ride (29.8 miles)
Found Loop (30.6 miles)
Eva Cranfill Ride (31.5 miles)
Martin's Store Ride (31.8 miles)
Waterworks Loop (32.3 miles)
Short Lower Yadkin Ride (32.7 miles)
Tour of Tanglewood (33.0 miles)
Tobaccoville All Hills Ride (33.2 miles)
Rockford without Rockford Ride (34.4 miles)
Liberty Church Ride (39.8 miles)
Lone Hickory Ride (39.8 miles)
Belews Lake Tour (40.0 miles)
Farmington with Pudding Ridge Ride (40.7 miles)
Flat Louise (44.0 miles)
Rockford Road Loop (44.2 miles)
El Oasis Ride (45.3 miles)
White Rabbit Ride (45.6 miles)
Lost Loop (47.1 miles)
Bear Creek (50.1 miles)
Short Rockford Loop (50.1 miles)
Lower Yadkin Loop (52.7 miles)
Rockford-Siloam Reverse Loop (54.6 miles)
Siloam-Rockford Loop (56.6 miles)
Tour Around Pilot Knob (56.8 miles)
Bakery Store Ride (58.1 miles)
Dobson Loop (68.0 miles)
Tour of Hanging Rock (69.5 miles)

People in the Know

If you're interested in learning more about bicycling and touring, here are some other good sources of information:

Division of Bicycle and Pedestrian Transportation
North Carolina Department of Transportation
P.O. Box 25201
Raleigh, NC 27611
PHONE: 919/733-2804
FAX: 919/715-4422
EMAIL: bikeped_transportation@dot.state.nc.us
INTERNET: www. dot.state.nc.us/transit/bicycle

This division is responsible for developing state bike routes and mapping them. They have also worked with local areas to develop routes within counties or regions. There is no charge for the maps they provide. They also have a lot of other information on cycling safety, education programs for cyclists, bike racing, and many other topics.

Touring Information
League of American Bicyclists
190 West Ostend Street, Suite 120
Baltimore, MD 21230
PHONE: 410/539-3399
INTERNET: www.bikeleague.org

This national bicyclists organization began in 1880 as the League of American Wheelmen. Their website offers information on touring, national bike rallies, education, and advocacy.

Winston-Salem Visitors Center
601 North Cherry Street
Winston-Salem, NC 27101
336/777-3796

The visitors center will welcome you with coffee, cookies, and information about points of interest in the area. In addition to providing historical background about the city, the audiovisual presentation gives a good overview of the city today.

Winston-Salem Convention & Visitors Bureau
601 West Fourth Street
Winston-Salem, NC 27101
336/724-6088

County Bike Route Map
Winston-Salem Department of Transportation
City Hall
Winston-Salem, NC 27101
336-727-2707

The Winston-Salem/Forsyth County Planning Department, in conjunction with the N.C. Department of Transportation, has produced a bike map for Forsyth County, showing twenty-five signed bike routes in the city and county. Where routes in the book overlap or intersect with these county bike routes, it is indicated in the ride descriptions.

Bike Racks on Buses Program
Winston-Salem Transit Autoority (WSTA)
100 West Fifth Street
Winston-Salem, NC 27101
336-727-2000

In an effort to promote bicycling, the city of Winston-Salem installed bike racks on the front of all city buses. The racks swing out from the bus and can hold two bicycles. Using the bus gives cyclists more options about where to ride and helps you avoid heavily congested areas.

Help Us Keep This Book Accurate

The authors and editors have made every effort to ensure that this guide is as accurate and useful as possible. However, a number of factors can affect the accuracy. First of all, every odometer is different. We hope that the mileage indicated is within 0.1 or 0.2 mile of what you find. Secondly, many other things can change after a book is published: establishments close, phone numbers change, road names and numbers change, manmade landmarks disappear.

We would love to hear from you concerning your use of this book. If you find discrepancies, please let us know. We'd also like to hear about the things you like. While we may not be able to respond personally to all comments and suggestions, we'll take them to heart.

Please send any comments or suggestions to this address:

John F. Blair, Publisher
Attn: Great Bike Rides of Winston-Salem
1406 Plaza Drive
Winston-Salem, NC 27103
(336)768-1374 (in the Triad area)
(800)222-9796 (outside the Triad)

About the Authors

Judi Lawson Wallace

Judi is one of numerous cyclists who have benefited from knowing Ken Putnam. She bought five bikes from him over the years and learned much from that association. When she developed and taught an award-winning bicycling course for fourth and fifth graders at Summit School, she took the students to Ken's shop in Reynolda Village to see demonstrations of repair techniques.

As an advocate for bicycling, Judi won several awards. She received The Sam Thomas Award from the state of North Carolina and the North Carolina Bicycle Committee, which she chaired for five years. The North Carolina Bicycle Federation gave her the Silver Spoke Award for her activism on behalf of cyclists and bicycling. She chaired the Winston-Salem Host Committee for Bike South 2000.

A strong proponent of bicycling as a form of transportation, she commuted to work by bike for many years and used her bike to get around in Arizona, Alaska, and her native state of North Carolina. Since then, she has toured by bike in Arizona, Florida, Maine, Vermont, New York, South Carolina, Georgia, France, and all over North Carolina.

Her full-time job is communications consulting and training. She fre-

quently consults with the N.C. Department of Transportation about bicycle and pedestrian projects.

She is the author of *Short Bike Rides: North Carolina*, which was published
by The Globe Pequot Press as part of their "Short Bike Rides" series.

Ken Putnam, Jr.

Ken has sold bikes to thousands of people in and around Winston-
Salem in the more than twenty-five years he has managed and owned bike
shops. Ken's Bike Shop in Reynolda Village has been open and thriving
since 1981. He often participates in Sunday rides (knees permitting) from
The Oaks Shopping Center in Lewisville.

An enthusiastic cycling advocate and coach, he has organized and
managed cycling events for competition, fundraisers, and just plain fun.
Some of the cycling events he has sponsored and/or organized include:

· The Polar Bear Metric Century held on New Year's Day since 1975

· The Pizza Hut Biathlon, held since 1983. It's now called the YMCA
Biathlon at Tanglewood.

· The Hanes Park Criterium Bicycle Race, which was held annually
from 1977 to 1992

· The Moratock Fun Triathlon (cycling, running, and tubing), which
has been held annually since 1988

· The Dixie Classic Criterium Series, held on the first and third Tuesday nights from April through August since 1998

· Many Danbury road races

· The Biltmore Estate-McDonald's Bicycle Classic, held in 1982 and
1983. This was the second largest stage race in America during those
years.

Ken has been a United States Cycling Federation official since 1978,
officiating at many national events and over 100 local USCF races. He
even raced some himself in the late 1980s and early 1990s, but confesses
that he was never very good. He has been a supporter, sponsor, and/or

officer for the Hearts Racing Club since 1974.

He participated in the inaugural Tour Across North Carolina in 1977, riding from Murphy to Manteo with other cyclists under the auspices of the North Carolina Department of Transportation. In 1981, he rode with Gary Fleming and Greg Bean from Winston-Salem to Hilton Head in 23 hours and 15 minutes to raise money for the North Carolina Lung Association.

He and Judi served together on the Winston-Salem Bicycle Committee, which planned the signed routes that traverse Forsyth County. He also helped Bike South 2000 develop their routes through the Piedmont area. An avid cyclist himself, Ken has personally ridden most of these rides many times and knows them like the proverbial "back of his hand."

After collecting routes and creating maps over the years and dreaming of doing a book, Ken hooked up with long-time friend Judi Wallace to make it happen.

Index